Banks, Thrifts, and Insurance Companies

Banks, Thrifts, and Insurance Companies

Surviving the 1980s

Alan Gart

Lexington Books
D.C. Heath and Company/Lexington, Massachusetts/Toronto

Library of Congress Cataloging in Publication Data

Gart, Alan.
    Banks, thrifts, and insurance companies.

    Includes index.
    1. Financial institutions—United States. I. Title.
HG181.G36   1985   332.1′ 0973   84-48440
ISBN 0-669-09374-2 (alk. paper)

Published simultaneously in Canada
Printed in the United States of America on acid-free paper
International Standard Book Number: 0-669-09374-2
Library of Congress Catalog Card Number: 84-48440

Contents

Tables and Figure

Tables

Figure

Preface and Acknowledgments

Although many industries enjoyed a favorable year in 1984, the banking, thrift, brokerage, and property/casualty insurance industries endured some of the bleakest times since the Great Depression. Saddled with bad loans, government regulators placed 817 of 14,700 banks on a problem list, while the property-casualty industry suffered its worst year since the San Francisco earthquake and fire of 1906. The troubles within the banking and thrift industries brought to mind the whole issue of deregulating the financial industry and the fact that change had been so rapid that planners and executives may be having difficulty in coping with both change and uncertainty.

Structural Change: Mergers and Conversions

The merger trends of 1980–83 within the financial services industry continued prominently during 1984. Among the key moves were the acquisition of DLJ by Equitable Life Assurance; of IDS by American Express; of Harris Bankcorp by The Bank of Montreal; and of Flagship Banks (Miami) by Sun Banks Inc. (Orlando). Sun Banks Inc. also agreed to merge with Trust Company of Georgia, the first merger accord signed in the Southeast banking zone. Citicorp also received regulatory approval to acquire First Federal Savings and Loan Association of Chicago and New Biscayne Savings of Miami. These acquisitions followed Citicorp's prior acquisition of a troubled California thrift.

With mounting competition in the financial services industry, we can expect to see more mergers and acquisitions (1) as stronger institutions gobble up weaker ones; (2) as companies attempt to expand their customer base in an effort to cross-sell additional products and services; and (3) as cross-industry mergers increase as more and more nonfinancial companies decide to enter the financial services industry because it is viewed as an industry of long-run high growth and promise. However, in the merger process, greater efficiencies are usually achieved with staff cutbacks. This loss of jobs ends the myth of job stability and security within the financial services industry.

In 1983–84 approximately 100 thrifts switched from the mutual to stockholder form of ownership, some in order to remain as viable institutions. In regard to conversions, the thrift mutuals have one large advantage over the insurance mutuals in that there is a sympathetic federal government regulator that set up demutualization guidelines. The process of demutualization for insurers is far more complex. However, we are likely to see a number of these conversions in the latter part of the 1980s as the benefits of conversion appear to outweigh the detractions.

Technological Changes

Technological developments have also continued to bring fundamental changes in the financial services industry. The growth of automated teller machines (ATMs) and point-of-sale terminals (POST) have altered methods of approving credit transactions and have laid the groundwork for wider use of direct-debit systems, which will provide immediate transfers of funds, while taking credit out of the credit-card system. The use of the home computer is also likely to change not only the way we bank, but the way we shop in this country by the year 2000. We can now use the home computer for bank balance inquiries, funds transfer, bill paying, electronic mail, financial and other information, the purchase and sale of stocks, bonds, and other securities, ticket purchasing, the sending of messages, news retrieval, travel guides, and comparative shopping. This latter option could gradually help to change the distribution or marketing systems for financial services, as well as other products.

Coldwell Banker, the Sears subsidiary that is one of the country's biggest mortgage banking companies, is installing computers that will let its realty agents obtain mortgage interest rate quotes and financing for clients more rapidly. The technology should enable Coldwell Banker to update its rates quickly, allow buyers to apply for a loan using the terminals and should shorten the application processing time. This network, called "Mortgage One," is a private label version of Shelternet, the computerized mortgage system developed by First Boston Capital Group. The Shelternet system enables mortgage lenders in any part of the country to make their funding available through computer terminals in brokers' offices throughout the United States. Real estate agents and their customers can then quickly scan a number of different mortgage loan programs and determine which makes the most sense for them and for how large a mortgage they qualify. After the buyer applies for the loan electronically, the real estate agent can electronically track the progress of the application. The terminal also prints out the mortgage documents necessary for closing once the lender approves the loan application. Other companies such as Better Homes and Gardens

Real Estate Service and Realty World Corp. use Shelternet technology in similar networks that they operate.

Changing Distribution Systems

The old system of selling insurance through agencies is showing signs of unraveling as mass marketers, stock brokers, and banks have attempted to increase their market share. In addition to the home computer/videotex possibilities of selling homes and insurance, other examples of the potential for changing distribution systems can be found in the leasing of space in bank lobbies to insurance companies or agents for the sale of personal insurance lines. Also, companies such as Metropolitan Life Insurance took a major step into direct marketing of insurance with an agreement to sell their products and services through the Reader's Digest Association, Inc. This new distribution arrangement to sell insurance to Reader's Digest Magazine's 18 million subscribers would supplement the current sales force of more than 10,000 Metropolitan insurance agents. Other companies such as Provident Mutual Life Insurance Company of Philadelphia have taken a step towards supplementary distribution of insurance products in their acquisition of Continental American Life Insurance Co., which sells insurance directly to consumers via telemarketing. Provident Mutual also joined the ranks of insurers who have purchased stock brokerage firms with their acquisition of W. H. Newbold & Sons. Although the sale of insurance products by brokerage firms has been modest, it is expected to increase as more brokerage firms are acquired by insurers and as techniques for effectively cross-selling financial products and services become perfected.

Deregulation

The financial services industry, just like the airlines, is going through a turbulent period following deregulation. Although a number of inefficient airlines were forced out of business, it appears as if the consumer was the primary beneficiary with lower air fares and, in some instances, increased service. The consumer seems to be the prime beneficiary of deregulation within the financial marketplace as more products and services are available in a highly competitive environment. However, a record number of bank failures, a struggling thrift industry, disappointing earnings within the brokerage industry, and the worst earnings performance in modern history for the property-casualty insurance industry have brought about cries for reregulation. There are lots of financial institutions that are in favor of reregulation and the making of one group or another safe or protected from competition. Some of these interest groups are happily using the Continental Illinois crisis as an argument for their position, claiming that the safety of the banking system has been imperiled by deregulation. In fact, most of the bank failures and troubled bank institutions have had little to do with deregulation, but a great deal to do with making bad loans in the energy, agriculture, mining, real estate, and foreign sectors.

With no overall plan or national policy for either product or geographic deregulation, the large banks are making an end run around Congress in their bid for greater powers to expand into insurance, real estate, and securities underwriting activities, as well as a reduction in barriers to interstate banking. Although Congress has not been particularly helpful through the end of 1984 in granting these new powers, the banking industry has wooed state legislatures, sympathetic regulators, and has found new loopholes in the old banking laws. State legislatures have learned that bank deregulation is a good tool to attract more banking industry jobs. For example, Bank America Corp., Citicorp, and First Interstate Bancorp have attempted to take advantage of a South Dakota law allowing out-of-state banks to sell insurance throughout the country. The Federal Reserve has blocked these banks from offering the insurance so far. However, other states such as New York have proposed bills giving state-chartered banks in that state broad insurance powers. Also, state legislatures in New York, Ohio, and California have voted to give state-chartered banks powers to develop and own commercial real estate.

Interstate Banking and the "Nonbank" Bank

Interstate banking is developing amid confusion and conflict. There is a regional banking movement and a limited-service or "nonbank" bank movement. For many years, corporations from outside the commercial banking industry have been able to acquire or establish banks. However, during 1980 the giant banks began using the nonbank loophole to essentially attempt to establish a network of interstate consumer banks. The future of these limited service banks is uncertain. Both the Senate and House of Representatives banking committee chairmen have vowed to pass legislation in 1985 that would bar any nonbank established after July 1, 1983. However, some leading banking lawyers are encouraging banks to act quickly and set up these limited-service banks because Congress will be reluctant to close already existing entities. If Congress does not pass legislation in the first half of 1985, then about 400 nonbank banks will be in existence and the Congress will likely follow with legislation that will confirm that which has already occurred.

Regional banking laws allow banks to merge across state lines within a geographic region. Three New England states—Rhode Island, Connecticut, and Massachusetts—were the first to set up a regional system; Kentucky, North Carolina, South Carolina, Georgia, and Florida have adopted a similar concept in the Southeast. Utah also has such a law, and New York, Alaska, and Maine allow reciprocal interstate banking. However, even these regional banking laws are under attack in the courts as being prejudicial to banks from New York.

The Supreme Court agreed to review the validity of state regional banking laws, and this will delay some bank mergers and continue the uncertainty over the already confused future of interstate banking. At issue is the constitutionality of state regional banking laws that allow banks to merge across state lines within a geographic region, such as in New England or in the Southeastern states, but exclude banks outside the region from participating. The dispute over regional banking has placed medium-sized regional banks like Bank of New England Corp. and CBT Corp., which want to merge and increase in size, against money-center bank holding companies such as Citicorp, which have been excluded from New England's proposed regional banking arrangements. If the high court rejects the Citicorp appeal and approves the mergers, you are likely to see lots of regional bank mergers in 1985 and 1986. It is also possible that the Supreme Court decision may act as a catalyst for Congress to pass a bill establishing a new national policy on interstate banking.

Loopholes and the Regulators

On the subject of additional loopholes, Citicorp has filed an application with the Federal Reserve Board to exploit a section in the federal banking statutes that they believe would allow them to underwrite corporate securities and to engage in a wide range of securities activities. Also, Bankers Trust New York Corp. has filed an application with the Fed to house its commercial paper business in an already existing nonbank subsidiary.

Although the FDIC has ruled that state-chartered banks can enter the securities business and that all FDIC insured banks can enter the insurance, real estate, and securities businesses through free-standing subsidiaries, there is much resistance to this viewpoint in Congress and within the other regulatory bodies. The FDIC's actions only add to the confusion, whereby one regulator says that you can do X, while another regulator says that you cannot. Hopefully, the confusion and piecemeal deregulation will coerce Congress into passing comprehensive banking legislation in 1985.

Acknowledgments

I sincerely appreciated the valuable suggestions, ideas, criticisms, and comments made by professional colleagues who included David Melnicoff (PSFS and Temple University), Paul Shalita (Goldberg, Dickman, and Shalita), Kenneth Wright and Peter Keir (American Council of Life Insurance), Helen Raece (CNA), Albert Swanke (CIGNA), Louis Bell and Donald Whyte (Hamilton Reliance Savings), and Rick Wilhide (Wilmington Trust). I also want to thank Kathe Mengle who typed most of the book, and Lauren Cohn, Steven, Lisa, Deedy and Zelda Gart who helped type part of the manuscript. My family deserves a special thank-you for their encouragement, help, and support, and a special apology for the lack of attention that they received during many evenings and weekends while I worked on the manuscript.

Banks, Thrifts,
and Insurance Companies

1
Introduction

The financial services industry is undergoing a period of sweeping transition. In fact, the major challenge facing our financial institutions is rapid change. We are certainly witnessing a revolution when it comes to the changes in regulation, in technology, and in financial structure that are taking place among commercial banks, thrift institutions, and insurance companies. One prerequisite for productively meeting this challenge and dealing with change is effective management of people and information.

Regulation and Deregulation

Interest rates have been deregulated. The current battle that is taking place in Congress and among the regulatory authorities is over product and geographical deregulation.

We cannot overemphasize the importance of legislative and regulatory developments in shaping the future of the financial services industry (see chapter 2). Decisions in Washington on taxes, regulation, and deregulation affect financial organizations all over the country. It is Congress that ultimately will determine whether commercial banks will be able to underwrite and sell insurance and whether banks will be able to underwrite municipal revenue bonds and mortgage-backed securities. It is also Congress that will determine whether commercial banks will be permitted to eventually have interstate banking or whether the Comptroller of the Currency's recent approval of nonbank banks, alternatively called consumer banks, or demi-banks, will be allowed or voted out of existence in 1985. It is the nonbank bank loophole that permits large bank holding companies to open depository offices throughout the country as long as they do not offer both demand deposits and make commercial loans. Since a nonbank bank, or consumer bank, is not considered a commercial bank, it is not governed by the Bank Holding Company Act, which forbids interstate banking. Most small independent banks and thrifts are vehemently opposed to the approvals being granted by the Comptroller of the Currency for the establishment of these nonbank banks because they feel threatened by larger bank holding companies that could potentially operate on their home turf. They have been lobbying hard with Congress to close this loophole.

The Federal Reserve Board, in a November 1984 letter to Suburban Bancorp of Bethesda, Maryland, has imposed further restrictions on the operations of nonbank banks, a move some bankers say will make these banks unattractive. The restrictions prohibit a bank holding company from providing services such as check clearing, data processing, and check cashing at an office of a nonbank bank.

Regulatory authorities, such as the Federal Deposit Insurance Corporation (FDIC), seem to support allowing the 9,300 banks under their supervision to offer additional products. The FDIC has ruled that state-chartered banks that are not regulated by the Federal Reserve Board can offer brokerage services, including the underwriting of equity securities, through a bona fide subsidiary or affiliate. The big money center banks, which have been leading the push to expand the powers of banks, are not affected by the FDIC ruling and still are prohibited from conducting most securities business. This action by the FDIC is expected to be fought by the Securities Industry Association, a trade group that does not want to see the erosion of the profitability of current members that would seem to be a by-product of the FDIC's suggested product deregulation.

Also, the FDIC proposed rules in late November 1984 under which the 14,700 banks that it insures could enter the insurance, real estate, data processing, securities, and travel agency businesses. The FDIC proposal would let insured banks underwrite insurance policies and real estate transactions as long as the underwriting activities are conducted through a bona fide subsidiary. Insurance and real estate brokerage activities would be allowed in-house at the banks. Sales of securities, travel services, and data processing could also be made directly from the banks.

The bona fide subsidiary required for such underwriting business must be adequately capitalized, be physically separate from the bank in its operations, not share a common name or logo with the bank, and maintain a substantially different employee group. The FDIC proposal also prohibits a bank with a subsidiary engaged in insurance or real estate underwriting from conditioning any extension of credit on the requirement that the borrower purchase any product or service from the subsidiary.

These proposed rules would become final if the FDIC approves them after receiving public comment. The proposed rules would not immediately affect national banks insured by the FDIC because federal law prohibits them from engaging in insurance and real estate underwriting. However, state-chartered banks such as Manufacturers Hanover Trust Company or Chemical Bank could set up subsidiaries for these activities. Of course, it will be necessary for the states in which the banks are chartered to authorize the underwriting of insurance.

The insurance industry and independent agents have been in the forefront of the lobbying effort to keep the banking industry out of the underwriting and direct sale of insurance to the public. Insurance agents feel threatened by the potential loss of personal lines insurance sales to banks that claim that they can offer the consumer a lower cost of insurance because the branch system is a more efficient means of selling insurance than is an agency sales force. On the other hand, a number of insurance companies and insurance agencies have begun cooperative arrangements with banks to have their own sales forces sell insurance to bank customers in the lobbies of bank branches.

In a statement relative to underwriting of life insurance by banks, John B. Carter, chairman of Equitable Life Assurance Society, claimed that, "Banks should be kept out of the business of making lifetime promises. . . . The assets backing a policy have got to be there when it comes to deliver on that promise. They can't be in Argentina."[1]

We have already witnessed a breakdown of regulatory barriers to entering new markets. Many commercial banks and thrifts offer discount brokerage services, while some rent space to brokers, agents, and insurers for the sale of personal lines insurance to bank customers in branches. Certain insurance companies have acquired brokerage firms and limited purpose banks. Most life insurance companies make commercial loans in the private placement market and offer money market accounts with check writing privileges, while select insurers are offering "guaranteed" six-month to three-year certificates in order to compete with the depository institutions as the repository for insurance policy proceeds. Thrift institutions offer a variety of accounts with checkable instruments and are permitted to offer commercial and consumer loans, as well as credit cards, debit cards, and trust services.

Blurring of Functions

Banks, insurance companies, and financial conglomerates are adding as many new products and services as the law allows. Financial services companies, spurred by increased competition, have been squeezing through legal loopholes into new businesses. With regulations inherently unstable, there has been a push by institutions to break ranks and seek new lines of business within the financial services industry. There exists an almost complete blurring of the once-distinct functions of our financial service companies. JCPenney, Xerox, Greyhound, Kroger, and American Can—traditionally, nonparticipants in the financial services industry—have now become important players.

The proliferation of vendors within the financial services industry has made it more difficult for consumers to differentiate among products. The financial services industry probably could learn something from retailers, who do not distinguish themselves by products but by the image of the institution.[2]

Financial Conglomerates and Boutiques

Financial service companies are taking three different approaches to providing retail financial services to the consumer. There is the single-firm approach of Merrill Lynch, or Citicorp, where one firm offers all types of services under its own name. There is also the approach in which different financial services such as insurance, depository, brokerage, and real estate are available from different firms in one location. This is the approach taken by Sears and JCPenney. In the case of the Sears Financial Service Centers, the products are all offered by subsidiaries of the retailer and retain their original names (such as Dean Witter and Allstate). On the other hand, JCPenney has both its own subsidiaries involved in sales as well as joint ventures with other vendors.

The third type of financial service provider is that of the financial boutique, which provides a limited number of products and services but might target a specific market segment, such as affluent consumers or members of a specific ethnic group or association. Many institutions recognize that they cannot be all things to all people and have decided to specialize in some of the products and services they offer.

Chapter 4 examines a number of financial conglomerates (such as Sears, JCPenney, American Express, Merrill Lynch, Citicorp, Manufacturers Hanover Corp., American Can, Xerox, GE, CIGNA, Prudential, Transamerica, and ITT), and raises the following questions: Can there by synergy in such large-scale operations? Can the diverse parts of these financial service conglomerates mesh and complement each other? Do people really want to shop in financial supermarkets?

There are, of course, opportunities to consolidate operations in mergers involving financial conglomerates, which should help cut costs. There are also opportunities to increase the customer base and to cross-sell and mass market additional products and services. We can also expect additional cross-industry mergers as the quest for customers continues. Whoever finds a way to effectively distribute multiple-service products to a defined target market is likely to be a big winner in the financial services revolution.[3]

One essential skill for financial service firms will be the ability to undertake successful mergers and to achieve economies of scale. Economies of scale in financial service mergers appear only when management demonstrates "the tenacity to cut costs, to reduce staff, to make no foolish promises to those acquired, and to face the merger of technology."[4]

Capital and customers also shape the future of financial institutions. You must have adequate capital from a regulatory viewpoint and as a competitive weapon or currency that enables a firm to buy companies and afford the investments in technology and people.[5]

Technological Change

On the technological front (see chapter 3), we have seen the growth of automated teller machines, point-of-sale terminals, banking at home, the proliferation of home computers, the development of videotex systems, and the potential for the development of the debit card and the smart card. The latter is a credit card with an integrated circuit chip or a counterfeit-proof magnetic strip that should prevent "skimming information from a valid card's magnetic strip and rerecording it on another card." Hopefully, the use of the smart card will help prevent approximately $200 million in estimated fraudulent losses per year on credit cards at banks.

The technological system that offers the most potential for dramatically changing the way financial services are sold or distributed is the videotex system. The videotex service would enable consumers to use home computers or special adapters to retrieve news, information, special data bases, sports scores, encyclopedia pages, stock and bond prices, telephone directories; provide catalog shopping services, shopping and banking at home; place orders to buy and sell stocks and bonds; purchase tickets for theatrical and sporting events; place bets on off-track betting; make or purchase travel arrangements, read books and articles from extensive library collections; and perhaps review for the college board examinations by practicing on a few sample tests.

Although the consumers who have used the system have enjoyed it immensely (especially the comparative shopping features), many of the talked-about advances in technology will proceed slowly because they are currently too expensive for the mass consumer market and are driven more by competition than by consumer demand. High costs are an important concern limiting the potential acceptance of videotex systems. Despite the current lack of strong consumer demand, a number of industry players plan to pursue this market, some out of fear that if they don't act, Sears or JCPenney will be there first and attract their upscale customers.

There are some major players in various stages of developing videotex systems. In the forefront is Knight-Ridder Inc., the first company to market a videotex service. They signed up just under 3,000 subscribers in their first full year, compared with 5,000 that had been targeted in the southern Florida market. CBS, IBM, and Sears teamed up to form a videotex venture in 1983, but they are not expected to begin marketing a service until at least 1986. A competitor on the west coast in Southern California is the Times Mirror videotex system, which began marketing its service in 1984. Keycom Electronics, a venture formed by Centel, Honeywell, and Field Enterprises also opened a videotex system in 1984, while Citicorp, RCA, and JCPenney were discussing the formation of a joint venture to provide a videotex service in the mid-1980s. Also, the Chemical Bank may be adding some videotex features to its Pronto home banking system.

There are a number of key questions that must be answered that are related to the changes in technology. Can the costs to the consumer for using the videotex system be cut in half or can enough advertising or service revenues be generated to ensure the commercial viability of the system? Is there really a threat to the insurance agent from the fact that banks or videotex systems might be offering personal insurance lines to consumers at prices below those offered by agents? Also, why should debit cards and point-of-sale terminals become popular when the consumer can use a credit card and control the float?

Problems of the Financial Services Industry

Although the financial services industry is in many respects a growth industry, it is still bothered by the economic instability and interest rate volatility of the last decade and the deregulation of the 1980s. These factors helped create a huge consumer and corporate appetite for innovative financial instruments and services, and helped dislodge vast sums from the traditional resting places in low-yielding depository accounts or in low-yielding whole life and annuity policies. Consumers have certainly become more knowledgeable and sophisticated in financial matters and tend to exhibit less institutional or agent loyalty than they have shown in the past.

Our newspapers, magazines, radio, and television shows have been filled with stories of the failure, rescue, or forced merger of a record number of financial institutions. Seventy-nine commercial banks failed during 1984, the largest number of bank failures since the 1930s. This record number of failures came hard on the heels of less than fifty bank failures in both 1982 and 1983. In 1982 Penn Square Bank's reckless lending led not only to its demise but also contributed heavily to the interstate merger of Seafirst Bank into Bank of America in the following year and to the near collapse of Continental Illinois in 1984. Like many concepts in banking, "failure is not particularly easy to define because it requires the regulators to declare a bank insolvent, which in itself, can be a highly subjective judgment." To illustrate: The Continental Illinois Corp. was legally considered solvent, even though in a practical sense, the bank would have failed had the FDIC not come up with a multibillion dollar rescue effort to save the nation's eighth-largest commercial bank.

Just weeks after rescuing Continental Illinois, officials of the Federal Home Loan Bank Board helped oust the management at deeply troubled Financial Corp. of America, the owner of American Savings, the nation's largest thrift organization. The problems at American Savings were different from those at Continental Bank. Continental made poor credit judgments on a large portion of its energy portfolio, and when these loan losses and potential losses on the international front were revealed to the public, there was a run on the bank by Continental's large depositors. The run finally stopped when the FDIC guaranteed all deposits, even those in excess of $100,000. Even then, some deposit losses continued for a time.

Although there were credit problems at American Savings, the largest thrift institution in the United States, there had been a significant and costly gamble on the direction of interest rates and some accounting problems related to the booking of fee income and the treatment of repurchase agreements. Essentially, American Savings took interest rate risks in the futures market.

American Savings does not have an exclusive lock on thrift industry problems. The ranks of savings and loans are thinning, even though total asset growth has risen substantially in the last few years. In the mid-1970s there were close to 4,800 savings and loans, while at the end of 1984, the total was somewhere between 3,300 and 3,400: This means that close to 1,500 savings and loans were closed or forced to merge. Although the current failure rate is far below that of the 1980 to 1983 crisis years, about one-third of the remaining thrifts are still unprofitable. The problem lies in the maturity and rate mismatch between assets and liabilities. The heavy burden of old, fixed-rate mortgages kept the average yield on the thrift industry's loan portfolio at close to 10.75 percent, while the average cost of funds was approximately 9.60 percent at the time of this writing. Although there was a positive spread of about 115 basis points, it is not enough to offset operating and other noninterest expenses to enable the typical thrift to earn a reasonable profit. In fact, more than half of the thrift industry's total outstanding loans are still those fixed-rate, long-term loans placed on the books in the pre-deregulation period when few imagined that an 8 or 9 percent home mortgage would fail to cover the interest costs on a thrift's deposits. Today's ailing thrifts may be less able to withstand losses than they were a few years ago because of eroded capital and surplus and a much higher cost of funds under deregulation. The increase in market interest rates and deregulation in the 1970s and early 1980s has left many thrift institutions with a negative net worth. The deregulation of interest rates on deposits and increasing pressures from uninsured nondepository institutions forced some of the savings and loans to become more aggressive in bidding for funds and to take more risks in their lending practices while reaching for higher returns on these loans. One result of these more aggressive practices is a growing failure rate among small banks and thrifts and increased concern over their safety.

The insurance industry is also plagued by tougher competition and thinner margins. The property/casualty industry is really suffering from six consecutive years of underwriting losses. A number of the industry giants have begun to show quarterly losses on their earnings statements. This has dispelled the preconceived ideas of many who considered the business to have the characteristics of a cash cow (that is, a premium collection factory whereby investment income easily covered all losses, costs, and expenses, leaving a large residual for profits). The industry obviously has an overabundance of capital: too many dollars are chasing not enough insurance premiums. Excess capital has led to price cutting in commercial and industrial lines, as well as in professional liability insurance. The erosion of commercial line pricing has been one of the major contributors to the length of the negative underwriting cycle. Also, no single company has a dominant market share because the largest insurer has only a 9 percent market, while the ten largest insurers have a combined market share of less than 40 percent. Consequently, it has been difficult for one company to raise prices in this highly competitive environment because it is felt that any company attempting to raise prices could end up losing substantial market share and investment income.

Although property/casualty company failures have been minimal so far (thirteen small companies were declared insolvent by state regulators in the first ten months in 1984), the insurance industry has suffered two major casualties with the loss of Baldwin-United Corp. and Charter Co. Both companies concentrated on offering single-premium deferred annuities and were caught in interest rate traps and in policy cancellations. Most of the sales of these annuities were made through brokerage firms.

The once-staid life insurance business and its career agency system is in some cases suffering under the weight of its cost inefficiency and the pressures of intensifying competition. With conventional whole life insurance less popular, and prices of term insurance dropping drastically, new kinds of life insurance policies—universal life and variable life—were created to offer variable rates of return. Although it was not the pioneer in the field, Metropolitan Life Insurance Co. introduced a universal life policy in mid-1983 that is producing almost 50 percent of its new premiums. Skyrocketing sales of new policies are giving a sorely needed lift to an industry that in 1980 to 1981 was hurt severely by price cutting, runaway inflation, policyholder loans, and the surrender (voluntary termination) of old, extremely profitable policies.

The century-old and expensive system of selling policies through local agencies is being challenged, as brokerage firms, mass marketers, and banks begin selling insurance. The banking threat has acted as a catalyst in coercing the insurance industry to grow serious about cost-cutting and about improving the productivity of 250,000 insurance agents. A salient problem with life insurance, particularly for small companies, is that each new policy costs more in overhead than the insurance company takes in with the first year's insurance premium.

Banks, thrifts, and property/casualty insurance companies have not been the only financial service companies to suffer earnings problems. Among the financial conglomerates, American Express suffered some losses when its insurance subsidiary, Fireman's Fund Insurance Co., had to increase its loss reserves by $230 million. Also, Xerox, another big player within the financial services industry, had some earnings problems that were associated with its Crum and Forster insurance unit. CIGNA has shown huge losses at its property/casualty subsidiary. Merrill Lynch, another financial conglomerate, had a second quarter loss in 1984 and subsequently announced major staff layoffs and a reorganization.

The strains come from a period of high inflation and volatile interest rates; the inability to forecast accurately interest rate movements; a sudden end to steep inflation; deregulation; two back-to-back recessions; merger fever; poor credit controls by lenders who lost sight of quality control; suboptimal management decisions; a proliferation of costly new financial products; and not enough control over operating expenses.

Outline of the Book

In this book we are simply going to examine on a chapter-by-chapter basis the basic ingredients for change within the financial services industry. In chapter 2 we will examine carefully the changes in regulation and the impact of deregulation. This will be followed in chapter 3 by an examination of the impact of technological change, while chapter 4 will consider structural change. By structural change we mean the formation of financial conglomerates; the merger fever that has encompassed the financial services industry; the attempts to cross-sell products and services; and the conversion of mutual thrifts and insurers into stockholder owned companies. In chapter 5, entitled Some Problems and Solutions, we examine the nature of the problems of small banks, thrifts, and insurance companies and offer some suggestions on how to improve earnings at these institutions. We carefully consider adjustable rate mortgages, swaps, hedging, the sale of various assets, the control of expenses, and demutualization as potential techniques for alleviating some of the problems of our financial intermediaries. Finally in the last chapter, we examine future prospects and trends that are expected to take place within the changing world of commercial banking, thrift institutions, and insurance companies.

Notes

1. "The Peril in Financial Services," *Business Week*, Aug. 20, 1984, p. 60.
2. A. Furash, *Financial Services Industry Forum*, sponsored by Arthur Anderson & Co. and the Institutional Investor, June 3, 4, 5, 1984, Washington, D.C., p. 56.
3. S.H. Turner, *Financial Services Industry Forum* (see note 2 above), p. 38.
4. Furash, p. 56.
5. L.H. Kimmell, *Financial Services Industry Forum* (see note 2 above), p. 64.

2
Regulation and Deregulation

Professor Stuart Greenbaum of Northwestern University gave the following testimony before the House Banking Committee on April 11, 1984.

> About 10 years ago our singular financial system and the social contract on which it rested began to come unglued under the dubious banner of deregulation. Notably, this deregulation was not the product of an articulated public policy. It was not the implementation of supply-side economics or any other dogma of the day. Rather, it was the unintended side effect of an unintended inflation. It was yet another symptom of inflation's destructive impact on contractural arrangements.
>
> There is a need for public policy that respects legitimate property rights and the public's need for a measured institutional stability. We fashioned such a system in the 1930s and it served us well for 40 years. But, it has been swept away by the inflation of the 1970s. Its replacement has not yet been seriously addressed, and that is our highest priority.[1]

Depository institutions are regulated by an elaborate institutional structure that exercises extensive authority over virtually every aspect of commercial banking and thrift industry activity. A number of theories have tried to explain the proliferation of regulation in banking. One theory advocates regulation on the grounds that it ensures the honesty and soundness of banks and hence makes the economy more stable. Another theory disputes the public interest role and considers regulation as a means of protecting the banking industry from competition. A third theory is that government intervention in banking was motivated by considerations of public finance that enhanced the revenue generating capabilities of government authorities. All these theories of regulation have some merit. However, once government agencies have gained regulatory authority, they have been notably reluctant to relinquish it.[2]

The regulatory limits to banks' activities grew out of public concerns about the safety and soundness of banks and the financial system as well as about concentration of financial power. Current limits grew primarily from federal laws passed in reaction to the economic problems of the 1930s, which included the failure of one-third of the nation's banks.

Additionally, Congress sought to control banks' costs by limiting the interest rates that they could pay depositors (Regulation Q). Congress also sought to control bank risk taking and to limit concentration of financial power by limiting banking activity in the securities business. Another limitation related to interstate banking had been passed earlier. The restrictions on interstate banking are largely responsible for the existence of more than 14,000 commercial banks in the United States. Each of the limitations served to insulate financial firms from price, product, or geographic competition. These limitations, combined with prohibitions against certain real estate and insurance activities, served to keep commercial banks specialized in the deposit-taking and lending business until activity restrictions began to fall in the early 1970s. Legislative walls that had partitioned the U.S. financial system into separate commercial banking, savings and mortgage lending, insurance, investment banking, and nonfinancial segments have eroded during the past several years and appear likely to continue to crumble.[3]

Of course, legal and market conditions have changed since the Depression era. The Depository Institutions Deregulation Committee has removed most interest rate ceilings on deposits. Also, geographic restraints imposed by the McFadden and Douglas Acts and by state laws are breaking down, primarily because of bank holding company activities, states' reciprocal banking laws, and regulatory approval given for acquisitions across state lines of troubled financial institutions. In addition, product restraints are being severely tested with the growth of nondepository institutions such as Sears, American Express, Prudential, and Merrill Lynch, all offering some form of money market account with check writing privileges. The product regulations imposed on commercial banks were designed to preserve the safety and soundness of the banking system and to prevent undue concentration of financial power. Fears were centered on the increased risk that some assume to be associated with banks' expanding product offerings. Also, the fear of concentrated financial power seems to be related to concern that concentration of financial resources through banks' product diversification could lead to a misallocation of economic resource: "[A]s the division between banking and commerce erodes, banks may gain power to earn excess profits and to allocate credit on the basis of their own ownership interest rather than on an unbiased view of the investments undertaken."[4] A look at the salient banking legislation of the last two decades will reveal its impact on the issues of deregulation.

The Hunt Commission and the DIDMCA

In 1971 the President's Commission on Financial Structure and Regulation (Hunt Commission) recommended that thrifts be allowed to:[5]

1. Offer checking account services;
2. Remove Regulation Q interest ceilings for select deposits;

3. Remove geographic restrictions on lending activities;
4. Make consumer and construction loans; and
5. Extend the maturity of their liabilities.

Many of these recommendations were incorporated into the Depository Institutions Deregulation and Monetary Control Act of 1980 (DIDMCA). The major features in the DIDMCA included:

1. Eliminating interest rate ceilings on deposits by March 1, 1986;
2. Allowing all depository institutions to offer NOW accounts;
3. Offering Federal Reserve services to member and nonmember institutions on an equal basis;
4. Opening the discount window at the Federal Reserve to all depository institutions;
5. Subjecting all depository institutions offering transaction accounts to universal reserve requirements set by the central bank;
6. Permitting thrift institutions to invest up to 20 percent of assets in corporate debt securities, commercial paper, and consumer loans;
7. Removing state usury ceilings on mortgage rates for three years; and
8. Raising the insurance coverage from $40,000 to $100,000 for deposits insured by the FDIC, FSLIC, and NCUA.

When the DIDMCA was signed by President Carter on March 31, 1980, Senator William A. Proxmire, chairman of the Senate Committee on Banking, Housing, and Urban Affairs, described the bill as the most significant legislation since the passage of the Federal Reserve Act of 1913, while Representative Henry S. Reuss, chairman of the House Committee on Banking, Housing, and Urban Affairs, called it the most significant passage of financial legislation since the 1930s.

The DIDMCA resolved some problems germane to the structure of financial institutions, gradually phased out interest rate ceilings at depository institutions, and broadened asset powers for thrift institutions. Essentially, the act provided for the orderly phase out and ultimate elimination of interest rate ceilings at depository institutions by 1986. Congress had concluded that limitations on interest rates payable on deposits discouraged people from saving money, created inequities for depositors, impeded the ability of depository institutions to compete for funds, and did not achieve the purpose of providing an even and consistent flow of funds for home mortgage lending. Congress also wanted the small depositor to be able to receive a fair market rate of interest. What Congress did not consider carefully enough was how mortgage lending rates would be affected by the elimination of Regulation Q. In essence, the subsidization of mortgage loans by relatively inexpensive consumer deposits was brought to an end with the deregulation of interest

Table 2–1
Steps in the Phase-Out of Regulation Q

Effective Date of Change	Nature of Change
June 1978	Money market certificates established with minimum denomination of $10,000, 26-week maturity, and ceiling rates based on the 6-month treasury bill rate.
November 1978	Automatic transfer service (ATS) savings account created, allowing funds to be transferred automatically from savings to checking account when needed.
June 1979	Small saver certificates established with no minimum denomination, maturity of 30 months or more, and ceiling rates based on the yield on 2½-year treasury securities, with maximums of 11.75 percent at commercial banks and 12.00 percent at thrifts.
June 2, 1980	Ceiling rates on small saver certificates relative to yield on 2½-year treasury securities raised 50 basis points (maximums retained).
June 5, 1980	Maximum ceiling rate on money market certificates raised to the 6-month treasury bill rate plus 25 basis points when the bill rate is above 8.75 percent. Other ceilings apply below 8.75 percent.
January 1, 1981	NOW accounts permitted nationwide. On the previous day, ceiling rates on NOW and ATS accounts set at 5.25 percent.
August 1, 1981	Caps on small saver certificates of 11.75 percent at commercial banks and 12.00 percent at thrifts eliminated. Ceiling rates fluctuate with 2½-year treasury security yields.
October 1, 1981	Adopted rules for the All Savers Certificates specified in the Economic Recovery Act of 1981.
December 1, 1981	New category of IRA/Keogh accounts created with minimum maturity of 1½ years, no regulated interest rate ceiling, and no minimum denomination.
May 1, 1982	New time deposit created with no interest rate ceiling, a required denomination of $500 (but no specified minimum), and an initial minimum maturity of 3½ years. New short-term deposit instrument created with a $7,500 minimum denomination, 91-day maturity, and a ceiling rate tied to the 91-day treasury bill discount rate. Maturity range of small saver certificate adjusted to 30–42 months.
September 1, 1982	New deposit account (7- to 31-day account) created with ceiling rate based on 91-day treasury bill discount rate, minimum daily balance of $20,000, and either a fixed term or a required notice period of 7 to 31 days.
December 14, 1982	Money market deposit account (MMDA) created with minimum balance of not less than $2,500, no interest ceiling, no minimum maturity, up to six transfers per month (no more than three by draft), and unlimited withdrawals by mail, messenger or in person.

January 5, 1983	Super NOW account created with same features as the MMDA, except that unlimited transfers are permitted.
	Interest rate ceiling eliminated and minimum denomination reduced to $2,500 on 7- to 31-day account.
April 1, 1983	Minimum denomination reduced to $2,500 on 91-day accounts and money market certificates of less than $100,000.
October 1, 1983	Minimum maturity on small saver certificates reduced to 18 months.
	All interest rate ceilings eliminated except those on passbook savings and regular NOW accounts. Minimum denomination of $2,500 established for time deposits with maturities of 31 days or less (below this minimum, passbook savings rates apply).
January 1, 1984	Rate differential between commercial banks and thrifts on passbook savings accounts and 7- to 31-day time deposits of less than $2,500 eliminated. All depository institutions may now pay a maximum of 5.50 percent.
January 1, 1985	Minimum denominations on MMDAs, Super NOWs, and 7- to 31-day ceiling-free time deposits will be reduced to $1,000.
January 1, 1986	Minimum denominations on MMDAs, Super NOWs, and 7- to 31-day ceiling-free time deposits will be eliminated.

Source: Federal Reserve Bank of St. Louis

rates. Congress also did not carefully consider the impact of deregulation on many small banks and thrifts in regard to major increases in their cost of funds. At the same time, many of the smaller commercial banks and most thrift institutions were caught holding portfolios of long-term, low-yielding fixed-rate mortgages at a time when consumers were shifting their funds out of lower-yielding demand, NOW, and passbook accounts into higher-yielding accounts within the same institution. The bottom line was a substantial decline in profitability for most of these institutions, and in some cases failure or merger into other financial institutions. Although the problem of disintermediation for depository institutions was ended by interest rate deregulation, this has meant that the Federal Reserve's ability to slow down economic growth now required higher levels of interest rates than previously.

The bill authorized continued authority for banks to provide automatic transfer services from savings to checking accounts, establishment of remote service units by savings and loans, and offering of share draft accounts by federally insured credit unions. In expanding the powers of thrift institutions, savings and loans and savings banks were now permitted to offer credit card services and to exercise trust and fiduciary powers.

Perhaps the most significant impact on the liability structure of depository institutions came as a result of the Garn–St. Germain Act on December 12, 1982, when depository institutions were permitted to offer money market accounts for deposits over $2,500 free of interest rate ceilings. These accounts had a limit of three checks per month and three other transfers. Again, with a $2,500 minimum, Super NOW Accounts were introduced in January 1983. They removed the interest rate ceilings on "check-like" accounts.

On the same date, the minimum required deposits for seven- to thirty-one-day certificates was reduced to $2,500, and the interest rate ceiling on that account was eliminated. This was followed on April 1, 1983, with the removal of interest rate ceilings on the popular thirty-month consumer certificate. All interest ceilings were removed on deposits maturing in over thirty-one days in October 1983. At the same time, early withdrawal penalties were reduced. All minimum deposit levels for IRA or Keogh investments were eliminated in December 1983, while interest rate differentials between banks and thrifts were removed on January 1984. On that date, thrifts were also permitted to place up to 10 percent of their assets in commercial loans. A year later, on January 1, 1985, the minimum deposit required in money market accounts was reduced from $2,500 to $1,000. Even this $1,000 minimum is scheduled to be removed on January 1, 1986. The DIDCMA also mandated that all interest rate controls be eliminated by March 1, 1986 (see table 2–1).

The Garn–St. Germain Act

The Garn–St. Germain Depository Institutions Act of 1982 and the DIDMCA of 1980 were among the two most important pieces of legislation to impact financial institutions since the passage of depression period legislation. Provisions of Garn–St. Germain included:

1. Allowing all depository institutions to offer a new account that was to be equivalent and competitive with money market mutual funds;
2. Removing interest rate differentials between thrifts and commercial banks;
3. Granting of permission to federal savings associations to make commercial loans;
4. Allowing federal associations to accept noninterest bearing demand deposits;
5. Expanding a federal association's investment limits on consumer loans from 20 to 30 percent of assets;
6. Authorizing federal associations to invest up to 10 percent of assets in tangible personal property (including, for example, vehicles, machinery, equipment, furniture and manufactured homes);
7. Broadening of powers of federal associations to invest in time deposits and certificates of other Federal Savings and Loan Insurance Corporation (FSLIC)-insured institutions as well as in municipal securities other than general obligation securities;
8. Providing for expanded capital assistance programs;
9. Providing for a federal preemption of state laws and judicial decisions that restrict the enforcement of due-on-sale clauses in real property loans;
10. Broadening the powers of the FSLIC, FDIC, and National Credit Union Administration (NCUA) by expanding the forms of financial assistance in dealing with troubled institutions;
11. Increasing the amount that can be loaned to a single borrower by a national bank;
12. Providing much broader authority for national banks to make real estate loans;
13. Expanding the authority for national bank service corporations to serve all regulated financial institutions;
14. Prohibiting bank holding companies from entering the insurance business as a principal, agent, or broker, except in grandfathered situations existing before May 1, 1982;
15. Providing federal credit unions with considerably broader real estate lending authority over maximum maturity loans for refinancing and with an ability to lend on residential real estate regardless of price; and

16. Requiring the FSLIC, FDIC, and NCUA to conduct studies on the feasibility of consolidating the three insurance funds, the feasibility of basing deposit insurance premiums on institution risk, the current system of deposit insurance and its impact on the structure and operation of depository institutions.

As pointed out in a resolution by the House Rules Committee, the Garn–St. Germain Act was designed "to revitalize the housing industry by strengthening the financial stability of home mortgage lending institutions and insuring the availability of mortgage loans."

With the introduction of deregulated accounts enabling depository institutions to compete with rates offered by money market mutual funds, thrift institutions also received some asset deregulation and investment opportunities that would help them generate the earnings needed to support more competitive rates to savers. In addition to offering broader powers for thrift institutions, the authority of the regulatory agencies was expanded in order to assist troubled institutions. These provisions permitted capital assistance and broader merger options.

Among the most significant provisions of the act were the granting of limited authority to federal savings and loan associations to make commercial loans and accept demand deposits. The aggregate amount of such loans outstanding could not exceed 5 percent of assets prior to 1984 and 10 percent of assets thereafter. Loans to any one borrower were limited to the formula applicable to national banks, which was raised to an amount equivalent to 15 percent of unimpaired capital and surplus on unsecured loans and up to 25 percent for loans secured by readily marketable collateral.

The investment limits of a federal association were expanded from 20 percent to 30 percent of assets for consumer loans. Inventory and floor planning loans were also authorized in order to facilitate the purchase by consumers of retail goods. In addition, associations were permitted to invest up to 10 percent of assets in tangible personal property, including, for example, equipment, machinery, furniture, vehicles, and manufactured homes. An association's ability to invest in real estate loans secured by nonresidential real estate was increased from 20 percent to 40 percent of assets, while associations no longer needed to confine their certificate of deposit purchases to those of FDIC-insured commercial banks. They were also permitted to invest in time deposits and certificates of deposit of other accounts of FSLIC-insured institutions.

Restrictions that limited savings and loan investment in municipal securities to only general obligation issues were expanded to include all types of state and local government obligations. With the exception of general obligation issues, a 10 percent of capital and surplus investment limitation was placed on the obligations of any one issuer.

Partial Deregulation

The DIDCMA and the Garn–St. Germain Act have helped to bring about the partial deregulation of the banking industry. Deposit rate deregulation was essentially completed with the removal of Regulation Q. However, aside from the spread of such banking products as money market deposit accounts and discount brokers, and the acquisition across interstate lines of a few distressed depository institutions, commercial banks have really had little significant product or geographic deregulation. However, there are currently pressures being placed on Congress by large money center banks for product deregulation, such as permitting banks to sell and underwrite insurance and to underwrite municipal revenue bonds and mortgage-backed securities. On the geographic front, Congress must also give guidelines for geographic expansion and define a bank which will help clarify the nonbank bank expansion issue, which is dealt with later in this chapter.

It appears as if the consumer demand for product deregulation is unlike the demand for interest-rate deregulation. The demand by consumers to obtain a better return on their money than depository institutions could legally pay caused a huge shift of funds to money market funds that offered checking services. This type of evidence of heightened consumer demand led ultimately to the deregulation of interest rate ceilings for depository institutions. However, product deregulation does not appear to have produced enormous consumer demand. It is doubtful that convenience alone will cause massive numbers of consumers to consolidate their purchase of services if financial products are deregulated. However, excellent service or competitive price may induce consumers to change their shopping habits.

Financial deregulation is confronting some tough political realities. The removal of interest rate ceilings and the unfixing of brokerage commissions have overcome the resistance of entrenched interests with the aid of a pretty strong argument favoring consumers. However, there does not appear to be much of a consumer constituency for product deregulation permitting banks, thrifts, insurance companies, and securities firms to get into each other's businesses more directly. Neither does there appear to be a pro-consumer argument to permit full interstate banking. However, there is strong opposition coming from industry trade associations, agents, and brokers, as well as some companies, to keep banks out of both the insurance business and the securities industry. Also, small independent bankers have mounted a campaign to try to stop full-scale interstate banking. Among the arguments being used is that the expansion of the money center and regional banks will curtail lending to small businesses. It is, of course, difficult to document this, but it makes for interesting political rhetoric.

The rescue of the Continental Illinois Bank by the regulators certainly has not helped the pro-deregulation group even though the problems of Continental had nothing to do with deregulation. However, the problems at Continental pose a serious threat to the banking industry's efforts to achieve equality with its competitors as well as a serious threat to product deregulation for the banks. The Continental fiasco challenges the assumption bankers make that the industry can handle expansion of powers. Of course, Continental was not a failure in the new powers area. But it gave banking opponents a major weapon. Opponents of bank product deregulation ask that if bankers cannot, with prudence, handle their own classic banking business, how can they handle insurance or securities activities?

Other opponents argue that financial dregulation has not yet delivered one of its highly touted potential benefits—an increase in the national savings rate of the public. Other opponents fear that if banks are permitted into other activities that there will be cross-industry mergers that will concentrate political and economic power. Another argument against deregulation comes from the regulators who feel that deregulation has caused the failure or forced merger of a number of small banks and thrifts. This was caused by an increase in the cost of funds of these institutions, which coerced management into reaching for higher-yielding, but considerably riskier, loans.

What then is the impact of product deregulation on the safety and soundness of the banking system and on the concentration of financial power? There appears to be little to fear from deregulating the financial products banks may offer. As a matter of fact, there may be benefits for bank customers.

According to conclusions drawn by the Federal Reserve Bank of Atlanta,[6]

> The appropriate concern when considering the potential risk of allowing an additional activity is not the activity alone, but how the activity contributes to total risk exposure of the bank. A review of the relevant literature suggests that some new financial activities actually have the potential to decrease the risk exposure of banks. The literature also shows that acquisitions of financial firms do not necessarily change the acquiring firm's risk.
>
> Management of the new activities determines whether potential risks become actual. Banks may already take substantial risks on their loans, securities, futures and options dealings, maturity matches and many other types of activities. U.S. banks engage abroad in many ventures forbidden at home. The evidence shows that U.S. banks have generally—not always—managed these risks competently. There is little reason to expect that managements will mismanage new domestic risks. New activities can be managed in a manner that will stabilize or even diminish risk to the individual bank and to the financial system. Providing incentives to limit risk is a crucial consideration. Today's deposit insurance and discount window arrangements actually provide incentives for risk by reducing the exposure of both depositors and shareholders. Adjusting these environmental factors to shift the risk on to the private sector would impose useful market discipline.
>
> Failure to deregulate carries its own risk. Firms offering insurance, investment banking and real estate services are already invading the traditional financial service markets of banks, while banks are constrained from offering these traditional products. If less regulated firms are able to attract signifi-

cant amounts of bank liabilities to less regulated sectors, the financial system's safety and soundness will be reduced. Ensuring both intermediation and payments is important. Although nondepository contenders pose little threat to either of these systems in the short run, in the longer run, larger shifts of deposits and payments activity into less regulated sectors could weaken the safety of the financial and payments systems. Allowing banks to compete more broadly might delay or prevent that prospect.

Proposals to broaden banks' permitted activities also have raised concerns about concentration of economic resources and competition. Overall, however, concentration, tie-in requirements and conflicts of interest apparently would be reduced, not encouraged, by the relaxation of product restraints on banks. Many competitors from several industries would be vying for financial services business. New entrances are generally more innovative and market-sensitive. This would increase the number of alternatives available, encouraging competition, and decreasing economic concentration.

Fears that cross-industry mergers will concentrate political and social power still trouble some regulators and economists. Policymakers lack hands-on experience with the potential structural changes resulting from broad financial deregulation and are not entirely sanguine about its ultimate effects on financial power. Laws limiting the size of cross-industry mergers would limit any natural tendencies toward concentration, if they exist. Size limits for merging firms would have to be considered carefully to ensure that they gave no advantages to firms that are already large and that they did not unduly limit firms' ability to increase efficiency by capturing economies of scale and scope.

Current laws, regulations and market factors serve to limit significant increases in concentration. The evidence suggests that concern about conflicts of interest and tie-ins are largely unwarranted. Users of financial services would be able to spurn financial organizations that demand unreasonable tie-ins because deregulation should actually increase, not reduce, the number of alternative suppliers of financial services.

Surveys indicate that users of financial services desire broader product offerings from financial institutions. The public apparently believes it would benefit from some removal of activity limits. This expected benefit must be balanced against broader concerns about safety and concentration, of course. We surveyed household customers on their reactions to broader powers. Households generally responded positively. Those in the lower- and middle-income groups affirmed a stronger preference for making a wide array of product offerings available at single institutions. High-income consumers place a premium on receiving financial advice and information from a broader range of suppliers. Some households expressed strong preference for a commercial bank as their full-service provider. Asked what services they would like to see added to banks' present capacities, consumers indicated a preference for insurance and stock and real estate brokerage services.

The Controversy over the Definition of a Bank

There has been some controversy over the Federal Reserve Board's definition of a commercial bank as well as over geographic expansion by bank holding companies and product deregulation by some security firms that are attempting to form banks. What is a nonbank bank and what is a commercial bank?

The Bank Holding Company (BHC) Act defines a bank as a financial institution that makes both commercial loans and accepts demand deposits. A nonbank bank is simply a financial institution that offers one of these services, but not the other. When the Fed reinterpreted the definition through revision of its Regulation Y, which broadened the commercial lending concept, and when it insisted that NOW accounts were demand deposits, the Fed's definition of a bank was challenged in the Court of Appeals by an unhappy applicant to form a nonbank bank. A short history will make clear the concept and implications of a nonbank bank.

In 1981 Associates First Capital Corp., a subsidiary of Gulf & Western (G&W), applied to the Comptroller of the Currency to acquire a small national bank in California. G&W proposed to spin off the bank's loan portfolio to avoid being classified as a bank under the BHC Act, since it would then not make commercial loans. Avoidance of the BHC Act whenever possible is considered advantageous, since bank holding companies are subject to regulation by the more restrictive Federal Reserve Board. The comptroller's office reviewed the application and asked the Federal Reserve Board for its opinion. When the Comptroller of the Currency received no response from the Fed, the application for the first nonbank bank was approved. (Prior to this, there were companies with more limited charters that could have been considered nonbank banks.)

The Comptroller of the Currency approved two other nonbank banks during 1981, which included applications by Household Finance and Parker Pen. The comptroller approved the first de novo nonbank bank in September 1982, which was to be opened in McMahan Valley Stores. Although the first few nonbank banks were established by retailers, several players in the securities industry such as Dreyfus Corp., the Vanguard Group, and J. & W. Seligman applied to charter nonbank banks and had them approved by the comptroller's office. However, the banking lobby howled with disapproval.

Until December 12, 1982, the Fed had paid little attention to the Comptroller of the Currency's approval of nonbank bank applications. However, on that date, the Fed informed Dreyfus that it would consider it a bank holding company if it offered NOW accounts or if it purchased commercial paper, certificates of deposit, or bankers' acceptances. The Fed was broadening its definition of demand deposits to include NOW accounts and its definition of commercial lending to include purchases of the aforementioned money market instruments. Since bank holding companies are not permitted to underwrite mutual funds, the main type of business for Dreyfus, Dreyfus did not act on its approval to operate a nonbank bank because of fear of problems with the Federal Reserve and the issue of classification as a bank holding company.

C. Todd Conover, the former Comptroller of the Currency, continued to approve nonbank applications until a request was received in early 1983 from Dimension Financial Corporation to establish thirty-one nonbank banks in twenty-five different states. Before the Dimension application, no company had owned more than one nonbank bank. The possibility of creating a company with interstate banking powers through the nonbank bank loophole caused enough concern so that the Comptroller of the Currency imposed a moratorium on any nonbank bank applications received after April 6, 1983. The comptroller hoped Congress would act on this matter and either expressly authorize nonbank banks or redefine a bank for purposes of the BHC Act.

Despite the moratorium, the Comptroller of the Currency continued to approve nonbank applications that it received before the April 6 deadline. On December 14, 1983, the Fed responded by defining a bank in the same way that it had informally told Dreyfus that it would. It looked as if the Fed had put an end to the growth of nonbank banks.

However, on February 22, 1984, the Tenth Circuit Court of Appeals in Denver overturned a Fed ruling that an industrial bank offering NOW accounts and making commercial loans would be a bank under the BHC Act. If the decision is upheld upon appeal, it would wipe out the Fed's efforts to control the spread of nonbank banks and would throw out the Fed's new definition of a bank that included NOW accounts as demand deposits.

The Fed then surprised the financial community and reluctantly approved the application of U.S. Trust Co. to convert its Florida Trust operations into a nonbank bank while declaring "although the board believes that approval of this proposal presents a serious potential for undermining the policies of the [BHC] Act, the board is constrained by the definition of a bank in the Act to approve the application." The authorized institution is similar to a full-service bank.

About a week after the U.S. Trust decision, the Comptroller's moratorium ended on March 31, 1984. About twenty banks quickly filed applications to form nonbank banks throughout the country. For example, the Mellon Bank filed applications for such entities in fifteen cities out of its home state; Chase Manhattan filed twenty-one applications with fifteen out of state; Security Pacific filed twenty applications with nineteen out of state; Chemical Bank filed fifteen applications with all of them out of their home state; Bank America filed thirteen applications with all of them out of California, while Citicorp filed eleven applications with ten of them out of their home state.

Meanwhile, the Comptroller of the Currency announced the approval of ten more nonbank banks, including four of the applications filed by Dimension Financial. It also reimposed a moratorium through the 1984 congressional session on additional approvals of applications filed after March 31. The reimposition of the moratorium allowed Congress some time to come up with a banking bill and placed some pressure on them to do this in 1984.

Why is a decision by Congress important? Nonbank banks represent a creative way around the prohibitions of interstate banking, as well as an opening for "outsiders" to offer insured depository services. The approval of nonbank banks throughout the nation would act as a further catalyst in deregulating the banking industry.

The holding companies such as G&W, Merrill Lynch, and Fidelity Funds that have bought or started nonbank banks all have legitimate purposes that do not impinge upon the central commercial work of the banking system. For example, Fidelity Funds wanted membership in a credit card association and an ATM network, while G&W wanted a charter to handle IRA/Keough and other trust business. Merrill Lynch wanted a nonbank bank to provide in-house processing of checks and credit cards in its CMA accounts and to have an insured money market depository account available for customers.[7]

On the other hand, the large money center banks appear to be making an end run around the rules forbidding interstate banking by forming nonbank banks, a potential loophole in interstate banking legislation. If the newly formed nonbank bank does not accept demand deposits subject to withdrawal by check, or if it does not make commercial loans, it is not considered a commercial bank. It therefore is not in violation of the McFadden Act or the Douglas Amendment.

Local and regional banks and thrifts are frightened by the impact of a Bank of America or a Citibank office located across the street. The smaller banks and thrifts fear their survival is threatened. Because their constituents are frightened, so are the local congressmen. This should lead to a bill that preserves the community banks and puts an end to the nonbank bank loophole.

Deposit Insurance

Even though Congress acknowledges that deposit insurance has provided many valuable benefits, the Garn–St. Germain Act called for a review of the role that deposit insurance (as provided by the FDIC, Federal Home Loan Bank Board [FHLBB], and the NCUA) should serve in a deregulated financial market environment. All three government agencies responded that deposit insurance performs a necessary role, but suggested certain reforms in the way it is administered.

The FDIC favored a deposit insurance premium that would vary with risk. The agency also suggested that the FSLIC be merged into it and that the entire supervisory framework be reformed with the FDIC surviving any agency consolidation. The FDIC felt that it should have full responsibility for examining and insuring all banks and thrifts.

The FHLBB also supported variable premium rate deposit insurance as well as the use of private insurance to encourage thrifts to reduce risk exposure.

The agency believed that thrifts should have more capital and that their owners and directors should take a more active role in controlling their institutions' risk exposure. The FHLBB concluded that any consolidation "should not be initiated without first rationalizing the functions of the financial regulators."

The NCUA suggested that credit unions' risks could be reduced if those that attract accounts over $50,000 would pay more for their insurance and if the first share of every member were not insured. The agency would allow federal credit unions the option of substituting private insurance for public insurance. The NCUA was also opposed to consolidating its insurance fund with the FSLIC or FDIC.

On the regulatory front, it is possible that Congress will eventually authorize the FDIC and FSLIC to begin experimenting with surcharges on institutions whose lending policies have a high potential for generating problems with credit quality or interest rate spreads. Also, it would not be surprising if the FDIC persuaded Congress to rescind the law that exempts foreign deposits from FDIC insurance premiums. If the latter exemption were removed, there would be an increase of about $120 million a year in insurance premiums imposed on a limited number of banks. This would exort a sizable negative impact largely on the earnings of money center banks.

Banking Bills of 1984

During 1984 there were two major banking bills. Included in the omnibus banking bill passed in July, effective October 8, are the following amendments:

1. Thrifts have greater freedom to invest in securities under a prudent person rule.
2. The borrowing cap for savings banks and savings and loans has been lifted. The old provisions enabled thrifts to borrow up to 15 percent of their assets or up to 35 percent of their assets if borrowings are from the Federal Home Loan Bank Board.

The Senate approved a bill in September that would have given banks broad new powers to underwrite and deal in municipal revenue bonds, mortgage-backed securities, and commercial paper. Representative Fernand J. St. Germain, of the House Banking Panel, sponsored a bill in the House that would, on the other hand, have placed a curb on bank forays into new financial services.

Both the House and Senate bills would have closed the loophole in federal law that has allowed nonbanking companies to offer banking services. This so-called nonbank bank loophole has allowed some bank holding companies

to operate across state lines, circumventing federal laws that generally prohibit interstate banking. While Congress ultimately failed to pass any 1984
bill relating to the competitive and regulatory framework of the financial
system, the chairmen of the Senate and House banking committees both issued warnings before Congress adjourned reaffirming their intent to enact
legislation in 1985 requiring divestiture of all nonbank banks that began
operations after July 1, 1983 (the cut-off date set in the 1984 Senate bill).

This joint warning is interpreted as a message not just to firms wanting to
establish nonbank banks, but to the Comptroller of the Currency, as well,
that going ahead with nonbank bank plans will be risky. The warning stated
explicitly that those who invest in nonbank banks not protected by the July 1,
1983, cutoff "will, in our opinion, end up having to divest no matter what the
cost." As of this writing, approximately thirty nonbank banks have been
awarded national charters since July 1, 1983. An additional 329 applications
are pending from forty-six institutions, all but one of which are bank holding
companies (and hence will require approval by the Federal Reserve as well as
the Comptroller). In May 1984 Mr. Conover imposed a moratorium on additional charters, to terminate at the end of the 1984 session of Congress. Since
Congress did not settle the nonbank bank question in that session, the comptroller returned to the processing of outstanding applications after Congress
adjourned.

Implications of Increases in Capital Requirements

One of the strengths some regional and community banks have at this writing
is that their stocks are selling at a premium to book value. In comparison,
most stocks of large money center banks sell on average for 75 percent of
book value. This difference in valuation can be partially attributed to the
large foreign loan portfolios at the money center banks as well as their greater
need to rely on higher-cost money market funds. If international loan problems persist, regional banks may experience relatively stronger asset growth
in comparison to large money center/international banks whose capital-to-
asset ratios are being carefully monitored by bank regulators. Regulators are
requiring higher capital-to-asset ratios and promising tighter enforcement of
these ratios. If that effectively takes place, it could mean a significant structural shift in power among banks—especially if some of these regional banks
also grow externally in a reciprocal banking environment.[8]

Large money center banks are not going to cross the country with sacks
full of cash and buy up all the small independent banks even if interstate
banking is permitted. The money center banks may not be able to penetrate
small, local markets; they may not even want to be in these smaller communities. It is more likely on passage of interstate banking legislation that

these banks would have operations only in major metropolitan areas. If the regulators required the nation's big banks to raise their ratio of total capital to assets, the money center banks would have to raise over $5 billion in additional capital, leaving these banks ill-equipped to go on an acquisition spree.

On the other hand, it is possible that some large regional banks may be interested in acquiring some smaller community banks and that a few select retail-oriented money center banks may wish to acquire some of the regional banks. Deregulation also has sparked a large number of mergers among small community banks. Mergers among smaller banks can increase efficiency, diversify loan risk, and allow larger loans to any customer.

Insurance Deregulation

In March 1983 the governor of South Dakota signed a bill allowing out-of-state holding companies to acquire state banks and through those banks to sell insurance out-of-state. Citicorp, Bank America Corp., and First Interstate Bancorp either bought a bank in South Dakota or applied to charter a new state bank in order to take advantage of the newly allowed insurance provisions. The Federal Reserve Board held up the banks' applications awaiting a decision by Congress that would establish what activities are open to banks and clarifying what federal rules apply to state-chartered banks. The Fed has called on Congress to enact major legislation redefining the financial structure.[9]

A number of other state governments have begun to discuss or have proposed legislation to permit state-chartered banks to underwrite and sell insurance as well as own insurance companies. The governor of New York is proposing legislation to permit state-chartered thrifts and banks to underwrite and sell insurance. Delaware, Michigan, and Minnesota have introduced legislation to allow state-chartered banks to underwrite and sell insurance, while legislation to allow insurance sales by banks has died in Washington, Maine, and Connecticut. Panels in Illinois and Wisconsin have begun discussing whether banks should be allowed to sell insurance. Banks will likely limit their interest in insurance to personal lines, including life, health, auto, and homeowners.

Banks will be looking for easy sales, and less selling is involved with homeowner's and auto insurance, since over 92 percent of automobiles and homeowners maintain coverage. The pricing of these insurance lines is also "book list or catalogue" oriented and usually does not require sophisticated agents to handle customers. Since banks are already in the risk-taking business in their mortgage, home improvement, and auto loans, banks and thrifts are often the customers' first line of contact before the insurance agent can even get involved. After granting a mortgage or auto loan, a banker can suggest homeowners or auto insurance coverage to the customer right at the bank. With close to 15,000 banks, 4,000 thrifts, and probably close to 60,000 domestic branches, there is certainly a large customer base and an enormous amount of customer contact at the branches and through mass marketing with envelope stuffers in monthly deposit and credit card statements of customers. An insurance desk in the front of a branch and appropriate advertising can also attract customers. Banks will also be able to put their new technology to work by selling insurance through their home banking systems that should be able to offer good rates on insurance policies to consumers because there will be no agent commissions and, hence, lower distribution costs. The potential for reaching customers, coupled with the outstanding reputation of banks for honesty and integrity, make the banking industry a potentially strong competitor for insurance companies, their agents, and independent agents.[10]

The entry of banks into insurance and the increased sale of products and services via the home computer or cable TV promises added competition for the agent specializing in the sale of personal lines insurance. If bank insurance service is offered at reduced prices, price-conscious consumers who do not feel the need for personalized insurance or financial counseling could become insurance customers of banks. Initially, banks are not likely to sell commercial insurance lines, since these lines are more complex and often require studied fact-finding as well as detailed presentations—the kind of work agents do best.

Insurance agents must emphasize to prospects and clients their pre- and postsales professionalism. Just as banks will use envelope stuffers, agents can do the same with billings as well as other target mailings. Agents can also work with their companies to tap large associations or credit card customers of retail stores by reaching those prospects through the mail. Also, nothing prevents insurance agents from having working relationships with a local bank. Those agents who sell only personal lines will probably have to consider moving into commercial coverages, group insurance, annuities, and mutual funds as well. These lines will help retain personal line clients. The independent agent must promote his or her value as an independent business person who gives the client freedom of choice and acts as the consumer's advocate in recommending a personally tailored mix of insurance products. In addition, total account selling should become more important, since any client who is pleased with the agent's commercial coverages is unlikely to take his personal insurance needs to a bank. Finally, the agent who can offer mutual funds, money market funds, and annuities to customers is likely to keep their personal business as well.[11]

During 1984 Citibank, Bank of America, and First Interstate Bancorp announced plans to lease space to insurance companies. Leasing enables them to gain additional revenues from subletting space and from receiving a percentage of sales, and it enables banks to observe whether or not customers want to buy insurance in a one-stop environment.

Just for completeness, we will mention that although the Garn–St. Germain Act outlaws new property and casualty insurance opportunities for bank holding companies, Citicorp was permitted to continue to sell homeowners insurance out of several insurance agencies that it owned in Arizona, California, and Missouri because of a grandfathering clause. It is also believed that Citicorp will ultimately become an underwriter for target markets, focusing on financial guarantees such as the guarantees of payment of interest and principal on corporate and municipal bonds. A financial guarantee in the insurance business does what a letter of credit accomplishes: it requires banking skills more than it requires insurance skills.

Although it is unlikely that banks will be permitted to underwrite insurance by Congress immediately, it would not be surprising to see banks underwriting insurance by 1990. In the meantime, it is likely that we will see linkages between banks and insurance companies in the form of insurers renting space in bank premises and banks selling insurance, while insurers do the underwriting.

As a matter of fact, Citicorp has a new relationship with Travelers Corp. Chatworth Funding Inc. has been set up to buy loans or loan participations from Citibank. Chatworth is able to raise the money needed to buy the loans by selling commercial paper that is guaranteed by a surety bond issued by Traveler's Indemnity Co. Because of the financial guarantee from the insurance company, Chatworth commercial paper receives the highest ratings from the rating companies, giving them a relatively inexpensive source of funds. This program appears to be a means for Citibank to remove loans from its books, thereby reducing its need to raise capital. Citicorp can also earn fees from borrowers for arranging the loan. This is just one example of a number of types of working relationships that can be expected in the future between banks and insurance companies.

Notes

1. From Stuart Greenbuam's testimony before the House Banking Committee on April 11, 1984, 98th Congress, Second Session.

2. F. Ward McCarthy, Jr., "The Evolution of the Bank Regulatory Structure, A Reappraisal," *Economic Review* (Federal Reserve Bank of Richmond), March/April 1984, p. 20.

3. B. Frank King and D. Whitehead, "Crumbling Walls," *Economic Review* (Federal Reserve Bank of Atlanta), May 1984, pp. 4–5.

4. *Ibid.,* p. 4.

5. A. Gart, *An Insiders Guide to the Financial Services Revolution* (New York: McGraw-Hill, 1984), p. 25.

6. *Economic Review* (Federal Reserve Bank of Atlanta), May 1984, pp. 61–62.

7. M. Mayer, "Non-Banks Are Non-Starters," *Wall Street Journal,* May 22, 1984, p. 28.

8. T.H. Wooden, "The Financial Services Business," *Bankers Magazine,* March/April 1984, vol. 167, no. 2, p. 29.

9. A Gart, "The Tenacious Contenders," *Viewpoint,* Spring 1984, pp. 5–6.

10. *Ibid.,* p. 6.

11. *Ibid.,* pp. 6–7.

3
Technological Change

I n a speech to the National Association of Urban Bankers in August 1984, John S. Reed, the new chairman of Citicorp, warned that banks must jump on "the technological bandwagon or they will be swept aside." He predicted that many banks will disappear as radical technological changes transform banking into a "new industry" as the "economic forces of innovation and probably consolidation aren't likely to be stopped."

Reed also predicted that the financial services industry, including banking, will consolidate along the lines of retailing into "large national financial institutions analogous" to Sears and a "large number of special-purpose institutions" serving selected markets. In addition, he suggested that credit and debit cards "may well become the primary delivery system" for banking, supplemented by automated teller machines to supply cash and electronic home banking for paying bills. Reed estimated that it cost $20 a year to service a bank credit card holder, compared with about $150 to service a bank customer using a teller. In support of this trend toward automated teller machines (ATMs) and credit and debit cards, Citicorp now has links to 1,500 cash-dispensing machines in thirteen states.

Most experts feel that there will be much greater use in banking circles of automated teller machines, point-of-sale terminals, banking at home via the personal computer, and debit and credit cards. There will be less need for full-service bricks-and-mortar branches. Allan H. Lipis, president of Electronic Banking Inc., claims that "if banks are going to survive, they must increase their transactional services and decrease their costs. The only mechanism on the horizon for doing this is electronic banking."[1]

Electronic Funds Transfer Systems (EFTS)

EFTS involves communication systems that use electronic impulses to facilitate funds transfers among accounts. Sometimes EFTS expedites the check-clearing process as with check truncation, while in other cases EFTS supplants traditional check-clearing systems. Examples of EFTS include:

Bank wire systems, such as the Fed Wire, facilitate the direct transfer of funds among participating institutions.

Automated clearinghouses (ACHs) are systems for transferring money between accounts using electronic check images. The check information is encoded on magnetic tape that is presented to a bank participating in the clearing house. For example, the local electric company transmits to the local ACH a computer tape that identifies which bank accounts are, by prearrangement, to be debited specific amounts on a given date. The ACH relays this debit information to the participating bank.

Cash dispensers are limited service electronic terminals at which customers identify themselves with an encoded plastic card in order to withdraw a limited amount of currency from their deposit accounts or preauthorized credit line without using a check or withdrawal slip.

Automated teller machines (ATMs) operate in the same manner as a cash dispenser, but also allow deposits of funds to accounts, fund transfers, and loan payments and confirm amounts in accounts. ATMs were conceived as a means of reducing teller labor costs and branch energy costs, shortening the hours in which bank branches would be open, and offering extended service hours to customers.

Point-of-sale terminals (POS) are usually associated with at least one of the following services: (1) check authorization/guarantee, (2) credit authorization, (3) direct debit, and (4) point of banking. POS facilitates direct fund transfers between customers and participating retailers in which the POS terminal acts like an off-premise ATM and enables the bank customer to authorize direct transfer of funds from their accounts to that of the retailer.

Debit cards allow a cardholder's checking account to be debited immediately and the funds to be transferred to the recipient's account. This differs from a credit card transaction where the customer pays for the transaction at a future date.

Home computers, such as an Apple, IBM, Atari, or other systems, consist of a video terminal, disk drives, and typewriter keyboard that can perform as a word processing system, utilize literally thousands of software programs developed for business as well as for game playing purposes, and can be linked to a home banking service and consumer buying service. Less-expensive EFT technology, changing attitudes of the consumer, pricing traditional delivery close to actual costs, and more-expensive alternatives to EFT will tend to make EFT more attractive and should contribute to significant growth during the remainder of the century. Interbank transactions and corporate cash-management systems have witnessed extensive growth. Most large corporations have idle cash swept from their transaction accounts into interest bearing accounts automatically, and practically all corporations have lockbox arrangements with one or more banks to accelerate the use of funds and to reduce mail float. A reduction in the use of checks and check truncation (bank does not return processed check to customer) should result, improving the payments system primarily through the elimination of the costly task of transporting paper.

As the perception of EFT as a delivery mechanism becomes clearer, local systems will begin to integrate and interconnect. Consolidation should occur among ATM and POS networks and among home information/transaction systems as well. What seems likely to emerge is a small number of competing ATM, POS, and home banking networks with the capacity to serve all banks that wish to provide retail electronic banking services to their customers. As all financial institutions gain access to networks that enable them to deliver services anywhere in the nation, the branch/terminal issue and the definition of competitive equality on a state-by-state basis should become meaningless. Defacto interstate retail electronic banking should eventually be confirmed by law.

Technological innovation is propelling the banking industry through a rapid period of change. Many bank branches are apt to disappear as automated teller machines (ATMs) and electronic fund transfer systems (EFTS) replace high-cost branch banking. Many of the "bricks-and-mortar" branches in existence today may no longer be needed by the end of the decade and could be leased or sold. New branches may even be reduced in size and resemble Foto-Mat shops or trailers. These scaled-down units are often referred to as satellites and offer only basic transaction services. Branch hours could be shortened in an effort to control costs.

Although some bank labor costs will be reduced over the long run by mechanization, mechanization in the short term serves as a defensive measure to protect against deposit losses in an age of EFTS. The heavy development costs associated with remaining competitive through mechanization could lead to the merger of smaller banks into larger ones. There will also be opportunities for some smaller banks to utilize the new technology without developing their own systems by participating as a franchisee of one of the large banks. For example, a franchisee in the First Interstate system remains an independently owned and managed bank but must change its name to First Interstate. All customers of the small bank can use their teller machine cards or cash a check at any First Interstate branch around the country. However, they cannot make deposits away from their home state. The smaller banks get a range of services for which they pay First Interstate a fee. These include marketing, training, data processing, and purchasing, all of which cost less for franchisees. Also, franchisees can use the First Interstate banks to expand their loan originations and gain loan participations.

Smaller banks may not need extensive mechanization if they offer differentiated products that include special personalized services. It should be remembered that many people feel uncomfortable dealing with machines or computers and prefer the personal service offered by some banks.

Technology will also precipitate fundamental structural changes in the exchange of information and in the way products and services are sold, marketed, and priced. While EFTS will be evolutionary with regard to the transfer of money, it will be revolutionary in terms of the exchange of data and information. Totally new marketing systems could emerge. Such systems would provide the consumer with a complete listing of product, service, and price information on a home computer screen. The consumer will be able to purchase most goods and services from the home using the electronic media.

The extent to which Americans turn to computerized transactions hinges on the regulatory climate, available technology, and customer acceptance of EFTS as well as the cost to the consumer for using home banking or of shopping at home systems. For example, there has been some consumer resistance to using pay-by-phone systems because many consumers prefer to have checks as receipts for payments made and to control the float. About 70 percent of the families in the United States have checking accounts today, and close to 60 percent of all adults use credit cards. EFT has a current market penetration of less than 15 percent. However, by the year 2000, EFT is expected to reach an estimated 50 to 60 percent of the nation's families, while ATMs are expected to handle over half the transactions in the banking industry by 1990.[2]

Our two national card systems, VISA and MasterCard, along with two strong proprietary bank networks have introduced a dual interchange program allowing a customer from Philadelphia to access a bank account from an ATM in Seattle. According to John F. Fisher, senior vice president of Bank One of Columbus, Ohio, the popularity of ATMs as a delivery system will begin to be replaced by home delivery systems that should begin to appear shortly. The delivery of services in the home by the year 2000 is expected to become the principal method of consumer banking service. Our society will see a new range of information services available in their homes that will be as rewarding as the entertainment services delivered today. Personal financial business is likely to be conducted from the home over a voice and data communications phone that may be linked to a home computer or TV system.[3]

The use of checks may begin to diminish as EFTS become more efficient and as home banking and pay-by-phone systems grow in usage. As financial institutions continue to add charges for their services, customers are likely to use EFTS because it might provide a cash saving and save increasingly scarce consumer discretionary time. Banks might offer customers a choice of two checking accounts: one in which cancelled checks are returned at a fixed charge; and another in which checks are deducted automatically from an account with no paper and no charge passed on to the customer.

Banking has been relatively slow in developing new technology because of legal issues of jurisdiction that have delayed the use of more electronic equipment. There exists the potential to provide instant execution for nearly all types of banking transactions at the customer's home through the use of a leased wire, a telephone, a home computer, or a personal transmitter.[4]

Debit Cards

The bank card industry has emphasized not only new credit card growth but the debit card that allows individuals to have funds automatically withdrawn from their savings or checking accounts. With the acceptance and subsequent growth of EFT systems, nationwide debit card networks have appeared. It must be remembered that debit cards give the float advantage to retailers, while credit cards give the float advantage to the cardholder. The customer will have to be convinced of the advantage of the debit cards or POS cards before they will switch away from the use of credit cards. This might occur if credit card fees were passed substantially to the consumer or if the consumer had to pay interest from the date of purchase on the charge card usage.

Indeed, if these kinds of systems evolve and organizations can communicate directly, one has to question the future of the banking institution as it is known today. There may be less need for banks to act as intermediaries in performing many traditional banking functions.[5]

The system of debit cards and point-of-sale terminals can be viewed as a payment service system that serves to settle transactions among financial institutions, retailers, and consumers through immediate electronic funds transfer from the consumers' accounts to the retailers' accounts at the point-of-sale. The use of point-of-sale terminals is therefore an operational necessity if the system is to operate effectively.

From the consumer's point of view, debit cards function very much as checks do, except that there is no float available between the time of sale and the time that funds are debited from the consumer's account. Their advantages and disadvantages are obvious. Consumers may prefer to use a debit card rather than cash mainly for the reason of security. However, most people would indeed hesitate to use debit cards when they can enjoy the float by using checks or credit cards. Why, then, would consumers be interested in using debit cards? The consumers would be more inclined to use them only if they are charged less for the use of debit cards than they are for credit cards or checks. "Pricing is the key to changing the consumer's attitudes toward debit cards."[6] The idea of debit cards being less expensive than checks and credit cards is certainly not at all farfetched, since service fees for both checking accounts and credit cards have been increasing and are likely to continue to rise, thereby allowing debit cards to be priced competitively.

The retailers' interest in debit cards depends on two basic factors: customer convenience and the price that must be paid to the banks in the form of a service fee. For retailers to be in a favorable position, they must be able to provide customers with convenient and reliable service by accepting all cards while at the same time obtaining a reasonable fee schedule from banks. Most retailers refuse to be charged on a discount basis, as they are for credit card transactions. The card-issuing institutions are left with no alternative but to charge the retailer on a flat-fee basis. While flat fees may appear to be unattractive to banks at first glance, they need not be. Earnings from flat fees can be as profitable as those from any other type of fee because banks can afford to set them according to the quality and quantity of services they provide.[7]

Technology is not a problem; the cost–benefit issue must be resolved. It is essential for financial institutions, retailers, and consumers to place considerable emphasis on the long-run benefits. Once a nationwide debit card system is implemented, transactions requiring checks or cash can be reduced substantially. There will no longer be problems of identification, fraud, or theft because all personal information will be electronically encoded in the cards.

In order for debit cards to be widely accepted, universal standards must be established. It may not be possible yet to establish national encoding standards, although ABA Trac II is emerging as a possible national candidate. The debit card's most important feature is that consumers should be able to use their cards throughout a relatively large region. Also, retailers must be able to process the transactions quickly and accurately.

As a starting point for identifying the potential market, the primary candidates for debit cards should be those classified as "convenience users." The debit card transaction generated by these users involves localized and routine purchases such as those at supermarkets, department stores, convenience stores, and gas stations. If the debit card is to replace the use of checks and cash, these users must be convinced of its usefulness.[8] Although convenience users are heavy users of credit cards, they usually pay the balance in full and hardly use the credit feature. In fact, some banks are removing the twenty-five-day grace period on credit cards to encourage the use of debit cards.

A 1983 survey by the Federal Reserve Bank of Atlanta found that two-thirds of major grocery and convenience store operators in the southeast either already had ATMs or had plans to install them on their premises. Most of the retailers felt that ATMs promised distinct advantages in attracting customers, reducing problems with bad checks, and expanding their range of customer services. In addition, the ATM was often viewed as a stepping stone to the point-of-sale electronic cash register terminal and the debit card.[9]

Grocery and convenience stores, as well as oil companies, have been particularly important in the development of POS terminals and the debit card because these stores cash an unusually large number of checks and need a faster and cheaper means of negotiating such payments and of eliminating bad checks. The traditional retail payment system has become a burden, with supermarkets spending huge sums on check processing costs. Convenience stores are also concerned with eliminating currency in cash registers, which should discourage robberies.[10]

Another study conducted by the Antietam Group of New Jersey to determine potential markets for point-of-sale transactions found that supermarkets, gas stations, and department stores were among the major advocates of such systems. Moreover, the study also indicated that at least 11.3 billion point-of-sale transactions per year can be expected by the end of the decade.[11] The results of this study certainly suggest a bright future for the use of debit cards.

Several major oil companies such as Exxon, Gulf, and Shell have already planned to establish their own debit cards and point-of-sale systems. For example, Exxon utilizes the existing ACH network for its system in Arizona, while Mobil is using its own switch located in Kansas City. Consumers are encouraged to use the cards by the cash discounts that will be given to the users.

Home Banking

The actual practice of home banking began as a method of paying bills by phone using voice transactions, but was quickly followed by bill paying using a pushbutton phone. The user simply dials the bank's computer and punches in the access code, the appropriate account number, the amount to be transferred, and the number of the account to be paid.

Home computers, however, do not have on-line access to the banks. Instead, the home user must access a home information/transaction service. Through this service, the user accesses a financial gateway by entering a code (see figure 3–1), and the gateway in turn accesses the appropriate financial institution. This sharing system allows smaller financial institutions to provide services without the cost of building and maintaining an independent system. The home information/transaction service allows the home user to access services other than banking. This availability of other services on the same system may be a windfall for banks for two reasons. First, home computer news and information services such as the Knight-Ridder system are appealing to consumers. Plans to have commercials on the system will help recoup development costs and add revenues. Many of the videotex services would like to offer home banking on their systems to make marketing their services easier, and the potential to share in advertising revenues could be significant to banks that have spent millions on developing their banking systems. Also, the variety of services available on home information/transaction services might

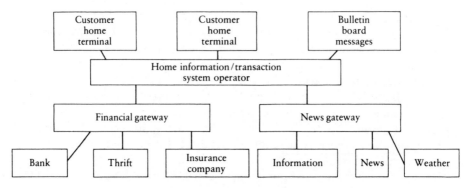

Figure 3–1. Home Banking Transaction Flow

attract enough users to make home banking services profitable to the banks offering them.

A standard of communication has yet to be established for home banking services in the United States. Most cable TV lines already in place are only one-way, but two-way transmission is needed for home banking. Telephone lines are in place in most households and will quite likely be used for home cable hookup, satellite transmission, two-way fiber optics, and a combination of one-way cable and telephone lines.

The main drawback to home banking is that although purchase can be made and payments can be authorized, the terminals will not have the ability to dispense cash or accept cash deposits. Also, the proliferation of home banking increases the need for security software and a cooperative legal system.

There is also a problem with equipment interfacing for home banking systems. New York's Chemical Bank can be accessed with Atari, IBM, Commodore, and Apple home computers. Another system uses the inexpensive Texas Instrument's TI-99/4A but also requires over $500 worth of accessories and software to transact with the system in LOGO program language, while Knight-Ridder's Viewtron system requires users to purchase a $600 Sceptre terminal rather than one of the popular and cheaper home computers. In a new marketing strategy, the Sceptre terminal can now be leased on a monthly payment basis. The company that first figures out how to interface with most of the existing home terminals and then implements a compatible system could have an eager market of home computer enthusiasts paying $10 to $12 per month for its service. Convincing people to buy expensive dedicated terminals, however, is a difficult marketing chore.

There are a number of brokerage firms that allow clients to invest through their home computers. Common to all such service is the need for a personal computer, a telephone, communications software, and a modem, which is a device that allows data to travel over the telephone wire. A partial list of the services available includes the following:

Unified Management Corp. (UMC) offers computer access to its six mutual funds without charging any access fees. With a home computer, customers can move money in and out of UMC's funds or even move money from a bank account into a fund. It is also possible to access UMC's central assets cash account, place discount brokerage orders, obtain stock quotes and account activities, and join an insurance-search program that evaluates your individual situation and finds the best value for your dollar.

Fidelity Investments has a service that lets you trade stocks, research portfolio and tax information, obtain stock quotes and the prices of Fidelity mutual fund shares, trade in precious metals, utilize the Fidelity central assets account, and purchase Fidelity mutual fund shares. Fidelity charges a $195 registration fee and an access fee of 40 cents per minute during peak hours and 10 cents per minute during off-peak hours.

C.D. Anderson & Co. gives twenty-four-hour access to its discount brokerage service, which includes order placing, portfolio management, and option prices. Their fees are similar to those at Fidelity Investments.

E.F. Hutton offers "Hutton Line," an electronic mailbox where you can leave messages for your broker, read investment newsbriefs, see your transaction record, and obtain stock quotes. The registration fee is $25 with a $17 monthly fee that includes two hours of computing time.

Dean Witter is expected to offer stock quotes, information on all your Dean Witter accounts, research information, and order placing. The registration fee is expected to be $25 with a $12 monthly charge. There is also expected to be a computer time charge of 30 cents per minute.

MCI Communications, one of AT&T's biggest competitors in long distance telephone service, disclosed plans for a national home banking system as part of its MCI mail program. MCI would like to take advantage of existing bank networks, particularly emerging POS systems. By tying into the switches that drive the networks, MCI expects to sign up at least 500 banks from among those already in automated teller machine networks.

MCI will provide two services, formatting payments data in the user's home and offering communications between the user and the user's financial institution. While MCI will format the bill payment and transport information to the bank through a network switch, the institution will make payment by whatever means is most convenient, such as by using paper checks, automated clearing house networks, or bank card networks.[12]

The MCI objective is to induce as many banks as possible to bring in the largest possible number of authorized payees for the bill-paying function. The MCI customer will be able to pay any bill, make bank balance inquiries, and move money around. This system complements MCI's mail, a postal system that had about 100,000 subscribers in spring 1983.[13]

If financial institutions or home computer service institutions can solve the compatibility, security, and profitability problems, home banking has a bright future. News services, computing and problem solving services, home catalog and purchasing services, and message services expand the appeal of home banking to the consumer. The idea of sharing the cost of the system makes it more appealing to the financial institutions. However, the banks need to keep in mind that where there is shared cost, there is also shared revenue. They need to know, in advance, the source of their profits and if revenues will continue to expand as more institutions go on-line with home-banking.

Videotex

The videotex concept is believed to have begun in the 1970s in England when the British post office began research into Prestel, an information access service. Videotex is simply a database with two-way capability that is designed to permit the accessing and rapid retrieval of specific items of information and the billing of customers using the system. Data are not routinely cycled in a broadcast mode. The individual user accesses the database as required so that access time becomes a function of the processing capacity of the host computer and the volume and pattern of usage.[14]

Although the videotex system was originally developed in Europe, the Japanese and Canadians, as well as several companies in the United States, have made significant progress in the videotex area and have begun marketing their systems in this country. The United States market probably has the greatest potential for commercial success because of the size of the market and the general fondness of U.S. consumers for electronic gadgetry.

The Prestel Club 403 service offers "Armchair Grocer," a British home shopping service that allows customers to order from among 1,200 grocery products and to have them delivered to the home. At current exchange rates, this service costs between $5 and $6 a month. It is coordinated by the Birmingham Post and Mail, a Prestel information provider. Also, Citibank Savings, the British subsidiary of Citicorp, offers telebanking services through Club 403.

The French telecommunications authority, PTT, has developed an electronic telephone directory. It plans to install up to 34 million terminals free of charge in homes and businesses throughout France. Unlike the Prestel system, the French system is transactional as well as informational. Another French development is a telebanking service from Credit Commercial de France called "Videobanque CCF." It offers real-time transactions plus "telecording" to download complete business files to micro- and minicomputers for use in cash-management programs. The service can also handle telepayments based on smart-card technology. Smart card is equal in size and shape to a typical credit card, but is embedded with a microprocessor that gives the card computer power or intelligence.

In Canada, there are a number of videotex developments. The initial service developed was informational and included weather, commodity and stock market quote data, as well as communications information. However, Le Groupe Videoway, Inc., a Montreal-based equipment/service packager, has developed an integrated home information system that is tied to cable TV facilities. It offers teleshopping, banking, and monitoring, as well as news and information services through a personalized multi-use terminal. The Bank of Montreal launched the first commercial home banking service in Canada in early 1984. Subscribers can currently access account balances, transfer funds, and view monthly statements, while subscribers will also be able to pay bills and have access to credit card balances.

The development of the U.S. videotex industry is taking a completely different course than it did in Canada or Europe because it is being developed by private enterprise. One difference is the lack of government support for the videotex industry; another is the lack of government-mandated standards. This has resulted in a wide range of activity with a variety of different approaches and emphases. Two basic technologies that have evolved: the alphamosaic method and the alphageometric method. The former method is used by the British Prestel System. However, its graphics capabilities do not meet the standards of many advertisers who are interested in a high-quality visual image. The latter method, developed by the Canadians, has much higher quality graphics but is also more expensive. There is no doubt that the consumer responds more favorably to enhanced graphics, but it is uncertain as to whether high-quality graphics are necessary or whether the consumer is willing to spend the additional dollars for better pictures. The answers to these basic questions will become more apparent as pilot and commercial programs mature and as the marketplace begins to dictate which technology will dominate.[15]

Videotex is a rapidly changing technology that should experience strong growth during the second half of the 1980s as the need for additional access to information and the speed in retrieving that information becomes more and more important. The next generation of videotex will include moving pictures of television quality.

As the home computer becomes a more and more popular item in U.S. homes, banks, retailers, and publishers have begun a tremendous push to sell services that enable people to make purchases of goods and services, check bank balances, pay bills, and even buy and sell stocks and bonds or purchase insurance without dealing with a broker, agent, or other person and without leaving home. However, these systems, which have the potential to dramatically change retailing and distribution systems within the financial services industry, are extremely expensive. The companies offering them (such as Knight-Ridder, Citicorp, Chemical Bank, the Times Mirror Company, Automatic Data Processing (ADP), Field Enterprises) are hopeful that there will be enough customers to make these systems profitable.

The systems that have been developed differ from each other. For example, the Knight-Ridder newspaper chain has a system called Viewtron that provides national news from the Associated Press to local news, any page from a Grolier Encyclopedia, a cram course on the SATs, the Scott Foresman reading series for children, the official airline guide, as well as nautical and road maps. Viewtron users can monitor their bank accounts, transfer funds between accounts, pay bills, make travel arrangements, and shop electronically at over 100 Florida retailers. The consumer can flip through the pages of a store's electronic catalogue and press a series of buttons to place an order. System operators control the computer link between households and the service providers who sell goods, services, and information, hoping to collect a fee from everyone involved.[16] At present, the system is being offered in Miami. If successful, Knight-Ridder plans to offer the system in five other cities where they own newspapers and in a dozen other cities where local newspaper proprietors have signed marketing agreements.

The publisher of the Los Angeles Times, the Times Mirror Company, also uses Sceptre terminals in their Orange County, California, system. The system is similar to Viewtron. However, the Times Mirror rents rather than sells the terminal to customers.

Honeywell, Centel (telephone company), and Field enterprises in a joint venture offer a system called Keycom to subscribers in Chicago. Although the system is similar to Viewtron, it does not require the special $600 Sceptre terminal. The consumer needs a $100 modem and a $50 program that enables a home computer to receive video pictures and to make phone calls.

JCPenney plans to become involved in videotex systems in order to stimulate catalogue sales through shopping at home. Penney has arranged a gateway on the Knight-Ridder system that should link shoppers directly to its own computer. The company would also like to sell its merchandise over other systems as well. It has a home banking system that it purchased from a regional bank in Minnesota and could sell its insurance lines through one of these systems. JCPenney has also become one of the largest POS processors in the country.

Chemical Bank and Citibank both offer home banking services. At any time, the customer using Pronto, the Chemical Bank System, can transfer money between accounts, check balances, and pay bills to New York area merchants that have agreed to accept paperless electronic payments. The system requires the consumer to own a home computer and to pay a monthly service fee. Chemical Bank has been selling franchises for a $100,000 entry fee, plus annual charges to other banks around the country that would offer the service in their local markets but would use Chemical's computer. Chemical Bank hopes to recapture a portion of its $20 million development costs through franchising Pronto. Chemical expects to add other features to its system in the near future. Citibank offers Home-Base, a system that offers at-home banking, a partial version of Dow Jones News/Retrieval, and bill payment to anyone; Citibank in most cases writes a check and mails it following instructions received from the customer's home computer (see table 3–1).

A group of close to two dozen banks gathered together by ADP, a computer service company, has begun to offer at-home banking, news, weather, and stock market information packaged by Times Mirror. Subscribers can choose between Sceptre and a Canadian terminal. There are of course other bank and nonbank systems that have been developed and are under development. The major problem is that the costs of providing the service to the consumer are exhorbitant; there are risks in whether or not enough consumers will use the systems and make them profitable. The sources of income will come from consumer subscriptions, advertisements that will appear with the news, and commissions on sale of merchandise and services on each transaction through the systems. Although some consultants are optimistic (Booz Allen & Hamilton and CSP International) about reaching multibillion dollar sales levels in the 1990s and reaching into at least 17 percent of U.S. homes by 1990, some system developers are afraid that the cost of providing the service will exceed what consumers are willing to pay as subscribers. Some executives fear that the inventors and marketing people have trapped senior management into investing in something simply because it can be done.[17]

Services such as news reports, stock market reports, home catalog and purchasing systems, and message services extend the appeal of home banking to the consumer. Newspapers and banks benefit from having these systems: they should both receive fee income from subscribers. For a bank, fee income that is not tied to assets is highly desirable. Also, banks can save on their own paperwork costs. To the newspapers, most of the information being provided to subscribers is already on their computers and can be fed automatically to the home transaction customers.[18]

There are questions that every financial institution must answer if it wishes to consider entry into the videotex market. Will you make a profit on the system or enhance cross-selling opportunities to your customer base? How much does the system cost and what are the options? A large institution might want to spend $7 to $10 million to create a proprietary software and processing system that might serve about a maximum of 50,000 customers.

Table 3–1
Comparison of Select Home Transaction Systems

System	Consumer Start-Up Costs	Monthly Fee	Services	Strengths	Weaknesses
C.D. Anderson	$300 one-time service charge; Apple, IBM compatible home computer	$10/month	Trading orders; Information: price quotes and track own portfolio	First home brokerage system; National in scope; Effective use of limited capital (no bricks and mortar); Uniquely suited to existing customer needs; well-targeted (17,000 customers)	Limited to market information/transactions; No advice/counsel
Prestel by Great Britain's Post Office[a]	"Considerable costs"; Television, telephone (no computer needed)	Unknown; Charges to call up certain information	Information	Government backed; Nationwide; Innovative (introduced in 1976; world's oldest videotex system)	No order placement/transactions initially; Costly; Relatively poor graphics: no motion or sound
Pronto by Chemical Bank	Modem ($75); Commodore, Atari, IBM, or Apple compatible home computer	$12/month; No charges for transfers/payments/time, on-line	Banking only: Account maintenance; Funds transfers; Bill payment (limited to 400 merchants); Automatic recurring payment; Checking reconciliation; Budgeting; Electronic mail (receivers: chemical; other Pronto users)	Low consumer start-up and monthly charges; Corporate commitment ($20mm development and marketing expenses); Innovative, "first in" operator; Collect fees via franchising; *Exclusivity*; only 1 bank on system	Services limited to banking; Monthly charge equal to Viewtron; Bill payment limited to 400 merchants; Revenues not commensurate with investment yet; Expertise required to coordinate/compete in fully dimensioned system in long term

		Information		
Viewtron by Knight-Ridder	Sceptre terminal ($600 or monthly rental) $12/month $1/hour telephone charge	Information Local news/information Educational Official airline guide Road maps, nautical maps, etc. National news Stock/bond date (E.F. Hutton customers) Dow Jones news/retrieval (+ $10/month) Banking Account maintenance Funds transfers Shopping Order from 100 + merchants, travel agents Scan pictures of products	Variety of services Graphic ability Collect fees from transactions/advertisers Locally oriented features	Numerous competing banks offering services to the same customer Fees paid to operator could be costly Upfront costs for consumer

Source: "Pronto" information booklet, Sept. 1983; *Fortune*, Nov. 1983; *Direct Marketing*, Jan. 1983.

[a]The introduction of gateways and Homelink (Nottingham Building Society and Bank of Scotland) will add banking at home, teleshopping, and therefore two-way communication.

Another alternative might be to buy the software from a franchisor while keeping processing in-house. This would cost about $500,000 and serve up to 25,000 customers. A third option would be to buy the software from a franchisor and use a service bureau to process. This should cost about $100,000 and also service about 25,000 customers.[19]

A bank also must calculate the number of customers necessary to break even and determine whether there is a chance of reaching this level of subscribers. Is there any chance of losing customers to the competition if the system is not made available?

The jury is still out on whether home banking and other videotex systems will become profitable or whether a financial institution will lose customers if it does not participate in one of the systems ready to be sold to the public. Test programs have indicated that people like the service. They enjoyed the up-to-the-minute news and paying bills through their banks. They particularly liked the comparison shopping. However, giving subscribers the price information they desire could weed out advertising by all but the lowest-cost retailer. Because of this, system developers expect to charge a small commission on sales made through the service.[20]

Insurance Industry Impact

These videotex systems are unusual because in the systems that permit computerized buying, the consumer is able to do comparative shopping. This means that the consumer can save a lot of time and money while letting the computer do the price shopping. In most instances the shopping service is able to find the cheapest price for a particular good or service. This service is extremely important because it has the potential to dramatically change the shopping habits of consumers and the way that we market and sell goods and services in the United States. In the insurance industry this type of comparative shopping could threaten the livelihood of some insurance agents who are dependent on personal lines' insurance sales to consumers. It is entirely possible that by the year 2000 most individual life, auto, and homeowner's policies could be bought without seeing an insurance agent by shopping at home on the computer shopping service and picking the lowest-price policy that gives the desired level and type of protection.

As a matter of fact, according to John Cox, the former head of American Can's extensive insurance group,

> access to the computer and the blossoming of the managerial sciences have given the industry unparalleled ability to instantaneously manipulate information. It will allow us to develop standardized contracts within easy reach of the cost-conscious consumer. It will allow the individual buyer to com-

parison shop, and it will make for increased efficiencies and increased professionalism in our distribution system.[21]

Cox has indicated that insurance companies are basically inefficient, with some companies spending 40 cents on the dollar between either distribution or administration of the underwriting and claims. Some insurance companies in an attempt to cut down on these expenses, primarily associated with agent commissions, will offer their standardized policies to the public at a considerable savings over current prices. Also, other insurance companies will concentrate on becoming more efficient producers and attempt to achieve economies of scale in their operations. This should also result in lower premiums for consumers. Since there will be little product differentiation in the personal line policies, the most efficient insurers, who have the most technologically efficient systems and lowest overhead, should make the most money.

Ralph Saul, former chairman of CIGNA, in the keynote address at the 1982 World Insurance Congress in Philadelphia, indicated that ATMs and two-way cable television systems are forging electronic links among banks, brokers, and insurers in a process of convergence that "could change totally the way financial services are delivered to individuals. . . . There appears to be little need for direct selling of personal lines."[22]

Among the 40,000 independent agents, the exclusive agents appear to enjoy a subtantial advantage, as far as automation is concerned, in that they interface with only one insurance company. It is easier to computerize an operation dependent on one carrier than one dependent on multiple carriers. Most exclusive agents have or should have direct computer connections with their insurance company. Nonexclusive independent agents will most likely find it a much longer, more costly, and more tedious process to interface with all of their insurance companies.

The computerized information systems and data bases built at life and property casualty insurance companies, as well as the use of word-processing systems and personal computers at work stations, have enabled these companies to increase the productivity of workers and to reduce expenses. Many clerical, accounting, and investment functions have been automated.

The insurance companies are now working on the interface network between the independent agents and the carrier. Agents should be able to enter pertinent underwriting information into their microcomputers and send the data directly to insurers for premium quotations. Insurers should also be able to use satellite data transmission and teleconferencing. The agent's microcomputer should then be able to issue the policy after the insurance company is selected. Before the end of this decade, the technologically advanced insurance company should be able to complete insurance transactions in an applicant's home via a personal computer hooked to cable TV or other modem.

Other Banking Developments

On-line computerization has replaced the laborious process of entering accounts in ledgers. Computerized record-keeping, electronic payment systems, deregulation, and toll-free 800 numbers enable banks to be less dependent on customers who enter the bank for their deposits, but have enhanced liability management and the raising of funds to support lending growth.

Technology helped to remove Regulation Q, the interest rate ceiling on deposits, and has played a role in loosening prohibitions on interstate banking. Inflation and technology essentially fostered the development and tremendous growth of money market funds, which at its peak had garnered about $230 billion from the banking system. Finally, under the Garn–St. Germain Act, depository institutions were permitted to open deregulated depository accounts in December 1982. With the exception of some modest limitations on selected accounts, Regulation Q has passed into oblivion.

The removal of Regulation Q has effectively ended the serious thrift and banking problem of disintermediation. Since depository institutions can now compete with money market funds and other investment instruments, the loss of huge depository bases during periods of high interest rates has been eliminated as a problem. The deregulation process has led to a relative increase in the cost of funds at banks as consumers have reintermediated or shifted their deposits from low-yielding to higher-yielding instruments. This increase in the cost of funds has led to substantially higher home mortgage rates and the end of the so-called mortgage subsidy provided by Regulation Q.

Lockbox Developments

Just about all banks have developed lockbox services for their corporate customers over the last few decades. However, separate banks were usually necessary in each city in which a lockbox was located. Five major banks (Bank of Boston, Centerre Bank, Philadelphia National Bank, Republic Bank, and Security Pacific National Bank) have announced plans to operate a joint nationwide lockbox network. They will operate lockboxes in Boston, St. Louis, Philadelphia, Dallas, and Los Angeles. This is believed to be the first nationwide bank alliance for lockbox processing.

The concept behind lockboxes is relatively simple. Instead of having remittances mailed to its corporate headquarters, a company instructs its customers to send payments to a post office box (called a lockbox). The post office box is emptied by bank employees several times a day. The employees deposit checks and forward payment data to the corporation. By setting up lockboxes around the country, the length of time a check spends in the mail can be cut, enabling the company to gain use of funds a few days earlier.

Although lockboxes have been in use for several decades, nationwide networks are relatively new. Banks traditionally have offered the service only within the same state because of federal restrictions on the acceptance of interstate deposits. This has forced corporations desiring multicity lockboxes to deal with several institutions once state borders were crossed.

A number of different techniques have been developed to give companies access to a lockbox network through one bank. For example, Continental Illinois collects receivables at eighteen locations and sends them by courier to the bank's headquarters for processing and depositing. On the other hand, rival First National of Chicago uses processing centers set up at five lockbox cities and deposits checks with correspondent banks. A third type of nationwide lockbox service involves an alliance among financial service organizations. Two noteworthy alliances have been formed by Equitable Life Assurance Society and Chase Manhattan Bank and by Sears and the Mellon Bank.

The five banks in the aforementioned alliance have chosen the name Imagenet. As the name implies, each of these banks uses image processing. This automated step is touted as being a faster, more accurate, and cheaper way to handle information because the process converts payment information on checks to a digitized format, enabling it to be edited on a computer. It is likely that the five-bank alliance will be expanded to include other key cities such as Chicago or Atlanta.

Productivity

Companies are pushing productivity, both by investing in technology and by laying off people. One visible sign is the 25,000 ATM machines installed in U.S. stores, airports, hospitals, and banks in the last few years. Companies are trying to achieve economies of scale, both by merging with similar institutions and by taking on new services well-suited to distribution through existing facilities. The vast network of electronic payment and computer retrieval systems have permitted leaner staffs and fewer offices. Sluggish earnings reports have also meant staff cutbacks.

Though the Fed introduced a national clearing system for check collection from all over the nation that initially operated smoothly, the continued increase in the volume of transactions has decreased the relative efficiency of tangible paper transfers. Electronic funds-transfer systems have been developed in which funds (in the form of intangible electronic imprints) are recorded on and transferred by computer. Automated clearinghouses process computer tapes rather than checks, while remote service units such as ATMs conduct many types of consumer banking services twenty-four hours a day, seven days a week without personal contact. ATMs and POS systems are facilitating the acceptance of debit cards by consumers. The debit card is inserted into a machine at the checkout counter and on completion of the sale, the amount of payment is automatically transferred from the customer's account to the store's account. Individual banks have connected their ATMs with those of other institutions to form local, regional, and national networks through which customers of any of the participating institutions may transfer funds and obtain currency. Systems have also been developed to allow bill paying by phone or by home computer. Additional features such as comparative shopping and the use of data bases and information systems such as those available on videotex systems are expected to show substantial growth once the costs to the consumer are dramatically reduced. Although videotex systems and the development of the home computer are still in their infancy, they are likely to play a big role in future payment, information, and distribution systems within the financial services industry.

Notes

1. "Electronic Banking," *Business Week,* Jan. 18, 1982, p. 74.
2. A. Gart, *The Insider's Guide to the Financial Services Revolution* (New York: McGraw Hill, 1984), p. 61.
3. J.R. Fisher, "Banking," *Proceedings on the Future of the Financial Services Industry* (Federal Reserve Bank of Atlanta, 1981), pp. 13–14.
4. Gart, p. 63.
5. *Ibid.,* pp. 63–64.
6. E.B. Cox, "Is There a Future for the Debit Card?," *American Banker,* Dec. 17, 1982, p. 16.
7. P. Limpichart, *Debit Cards: What Must Be Done to Promote Them,* Widener University Term Paper, April 1984, p. 4.
8. *Ibid.*
9. H. Stacey and W.N. Cox, "In Store ATMs: Stepping Stone to POS," *Economic Review* (Federal Reserve Bank of Atlanta), Jan. 19, 1984, p. 31.
10. *Ibid.,* p. 32.
11. M. Weinstein, "Retailers, Gas Stations Lead Point-of-Sale March," *American Banker,* Feb. 27, 1984, p. 2.
12. D.O. Tyson and R.M. Garsson, "MCI to Enlist 500 Banks for National Network," *American Banker,* Jan. 5, 1984, p. 1.
13. *Ibid.,* p. 8.
14. R. Wilhide, *Videotex,* Widener University Term Paper, April 1984, p. 51.
15. *Ibid.,* p. 7.
16. M. Mayer, "Coming Fast: Service through the TV Set," *Fortune Magazine,* Nov. 14, 1983, p. 51.
17. *Ibid.,* pp. 52–56.
18. *Ibid.,* p. 56.
19. Wilhide, p. 9.
20. Mayer, p. 56.
21. K.J. McIntyre, "Future Holds Many Challenges for Insurance," *Business Insurance,* May 26, 1982, p. 4.
22. B. Densmore, "Insurance Alternatives Changing Market," *Business Insurance,* May 10, 1982.

4
Changing Financial Structure

Historical Perspective

A trend taking place in the financial services industry is the formation of financial conglomerates that offer to the public the opportunity to buy a wide range of financial services from one company. Few analysts have stopped to ask whether synergy on such a large scale can really work in the financial services business. Can the diverse parts of these financial service conglomerates mesh and complement each other, leading to profit improvement by increasing sales and reducing costs?[1]

Some evidence suggests that it may be difficult to achieve these synergies. Previous attempts to create synergy in the financial services industry have been somewhat disappointing. For the most part, life insurance sales by stock brokerage firms and savings banks have been only modestly successful. Continental Insurance made little progress toward the synergy that was supposed to accrue from its Diners Club credit card operation or its consumer finance subsidiary (both units have been sold), while CNA Insurance had great difficulty entering the mutual funds business in the late 1960s. Also, Prudential and Xerox, which diversified into the property and casualty insurance field, have not been able to show an underwriting profit in this segment of the insurance business. American Express was not able to parlay its 25 percent holding in Donaldson, Lufkin, and Jenrette between 1971 and 1975 into any great advantage.[2]

Of course, financial conglomerates can gain significant cross-selling opportunities as well as increased opportunities for mass marketing of additional services. They also have opportunities to eventually consolidate operations and utilize available computer capacity, which can significantly cut costs. However, these synergies are not achieved overnight because one cannot simply press a button and make it happen. Although some mergers have been successful, many have ended up in divestiture. Nevertheless, the trend toward financial conglomeration is highly visible and likely to continue in the future as witnessed by the large number of nonbank companies such as GECC, ITT, Beneficial, Greyhound, Control Data, American Can, Transamerica, and National Steel that have become significant factors in the financial services business.

It is likely that the financial services industry will be considerably less fragmented in the future. It might be comprised of giant institutions, the largest of which will offer a complete spectrum of banking, insurance, and other financial services. As financial institutions grow in both size and scope of function during the 1980s, it may be difficult to distinguish between Sears, Citicorp, American Express, and Merrill Lynch from the standpoint of financial services offered. Financial institutions are expected to diversify even further as the giants offer more homogeneous, depersonalized products and seek greater market shares. These institutions should be able to provide individuals with basic services at a lower cost by avoiding duplication of effort and by utilizing new technology. However, there will still be room for the boutique or specialty company that will be able to carve out a niche in the financial marketplace by offering exceptional personal or specialized services.[3]

Some of the trends now taking place within the financial services industry include the following:

1. The distinction among the functions of banks, thrifts, and nondepository institutions has blurred somewhat when it comes to services offered to retail customers.
2. Geographic limitations to branch banking within the United States should diminish as more nonbank banks are approved by the Comptroller of the Currency and as depository institutions continue to acquire failing financial institutions across state borders. Also, technological developments are making obsolete the geographic restrictions of the McFadden Act. The bank holding company umbrella has also helped promote additional out of state business.
3. Many of the large banks would like to underwrite and sell personal lines insurance. While awaiting regulatory approval to enter the insurance business, some banks such as Citibank and Bank of America have made arrangements with major insurance companies to offer insurance to bank customers in select branches.
4. Some insurance companies have purchased stock brokerage firms, while some banks and savings and loans have purchased discount brokers. Others have started their own discount brokerage operations or have made arrangements to offer the service through an outside discount broker.
5. Some insurance companies actively pursue short-term commercial and industrial loans as well as longer-term private placements. Many insurance companies compete with bank trust departments in the management of pension funds, profit sharing plans, etc. Some insurance companies have purchased commercial banks and have established consumer or nonbank banks.
6. A number of brokerage firms and financial holding companies operate international banks and either savings and loans or nonbank banks.

7. Many savings and loans and mutual savings banks now make commercial and consumer loans and offer trust management services and discount brokerage.
8. The retail banking markets are no longer dominated by thrift institutions, credit unions, commercial banks, and consumer finance companies. Money market mutual funds and near-banks such as Sears, American Express, Prudential, and Merrill Lynch have offered keen competition in the consumer financial marketplace.
9. The entry of retailers such as Sears, JCPenney, K-Mart, and Kroger into the financial services industry represents another example of the move toward the retail financial supermarket. Shared branches where grocery and supermarket stores have started offering space to financial firms is another interesting approach to offering financial services. Kroger has entered into an experimental agreement with Capital Holding in Kentucky to open financial service centers in supermarkets so that shoppers can buy annuities and money funds at Kroger stores. Also, K-Mart has begun to provide financial service products such as insurance, consumer loans, mortgage loans, real estate brokerage, and other banking services in some of their stores through agreements with different vendors. JCPenney will continue to sell auto, life, and homeowners insurance through the stores and by direct marketing to its own credit card customers, as well as offer an array of banking services in some of their California stores. Sears has also set up financial centers in some of its stores in order to sell insurance, accept money market fund deposits, sell stocks and bonds, and offer home mortgages.

The potential impact of these near-banks on the financial markets, is enormous. Banks and savings and loan associations are still constrained by Depression era regulations that prevent them from branching across state lines, shut the door on domestic investment banking, or sharply limit subsidiary activity. Near-banks, on the other hand, are scarcely touched by such rules because they either do not accept demand deposits or make commercial loans. They are less restricted as to the business functions they can perform and the business locations they can choose. Also, many of the nonbanks have purchased, applied to purchase, formed, or plan to form their own banking subsidiaries. Sears, Prudential, Merrill Lynch, Dreyfus, Advest, and E.F. Hutton are examples of some of the nonbanking firms that are attempting to formally have a banking or quasi-banking subsidiary.

Merrill Lynch

Although Merrill Lynch is best known as a retail stock brokerage firm, it performs a complete array of investment banking services. In addition, the company offers extensive institutional and economics research to support its wholesle effort to buy and sell stocks and bonds. Its Capital Market Group is actively engaged in merchant banking, institutional sales, trading, arbitrage, block positioning, and underwriting.

The greatest growth at Merrill Lynch has come in its retail or consumer activities. Its money market funds and Cash Management Account (CMA) have attracted a plethora of new customers who potentially can become retail brokerage customers. The CMA combines a securities account, a money market fund, a VISA debit card, and access to liquidity through credit card or checking account arrangements with Bank One of Columbus, Ohio. The company also offers credit cards to its retail customers.

Merrill Lynch has also begun to sell insurance through its brokers in close to 500 domestic offices. Consumer insurance sales should increase once stockbrokers are taught how to sell insurance and to better understand insurance products and the insurance needs of consumers.

The company has become active in selling tax shelters in the form of real estate, motion picture investments, and oil and gas drilling limited partnerships. It also offers commodity services as well as investment and economic services to both individuals and institutions. The company has begun selling certificates of deposit (CDs) for banks and savings and loans, from whom they receive a commission. As custodian of the account, Merrill Lynch has created a secondary market for these consumer-oriented six-month to ten-year CDs, giving consumers who wish to sell, a quick, no-penalty exit. In addition to providing a new source of fee income, the sale of CDs has represented a hedge against a likely loss of customers from its family of money market funds when interest rates fall and stock and bond prices rise.

The company also has an active real estate subsidiary that offers to buy and sell homes and commercial properties. It offers relocation services as well as rental services. In addition, the company has entered the domestic consumer credit market by offering a revolving credit account secured by a borrower's home equity. The company will offer a line of credit equal to as much as 70 percent of the appraised value of the borrower's home, minus any mortgage outstanding. Merrill Lynch will also issue the borrower a special VISA card with a defined line of credit and a checkbook. Finally, the company would like to buy a savings and loan association in order to offer insured money market funds and to enhance the company's real estate activities, including the possibility of increased mortgage banking activities. All these services appear to be part of a corporate plan for Merrill to become a complete financial supermarket for investors.

Merrill Lynch has filed with the New Jersey Banking Department to form the Merrill Lynch Bank & Trust Company in Plainsboro, New Jersey. The bank will not accept demand deposits, but it will make commercial loans and will have full trust powers. In addition, Merrill Lynch has agreed to buy the holding company of the Puritan Valley Savings and Loan Association in New Jersey. However, this latter proposal may run into a permanent regulatory roadblock. Also, Merrill's application for the Plainsboro nonbank bank has been tabled by the FDIC to give Congress additional time to study the whole question of bank and securities firm relationships.

On the international front, Merrill Lynch has established an international bank, a merchant banking facility, and retail brokerage facilities abroad. It has also taken a large position in East Asian real estate through the acquisition of Fung King Hey's Hong Kong real estate empire.

Merrill Lynch has agreed to buy Becker Paribas. Its intentions are to keep only 200 to 300 employees, primarily in the corporate finance, debt securities trading, and commercial paper areas. This appears to be a relatively inexpensive opportunity to purchase parts of a failing firm that should enable Merrill Lynch to improve its position in the capital markets business. The transaction not only strengthens Merrill Lynch's capabilities in several key corporate and institutional markets, but adds Becker's extensive commercial paper operation, corporate finance department, and debt securities trading operations to Merrill Lynch's capital markets base.

Merrill Lynch has been innovative in its financial products and services. The CMA account, its diversification into real estate and into the sale of CDs for other financial institutions, its increased investment banking presence abroad, and the formation of a small bank in New Jersey, all indicate that Merrill Lynch has been in the forefront of the financial revolution.

The new bank should gradually take over Merrill Lynch's Cash Management Account credit card and check transactions from Bank One, saving the company nearly $200 million over the next four years. The company has raised its performance standards for brokers and is beginning to weed out the laggards. Also, Merrill has begun to attempt to convert the broker into a financial adviser at the hub of a network of salaried sales assistants and professionals who specialize in insurance, lending, and tax matters. At the same time the company is experimenting with ways to automate its services for the mass market.

These changes have come about because of the company's greatest strength, its retail system of 431 branch offices with about 8,760 brokers—which has also become its biggest handicap. However, almost all of Merrill's offerings are funneled through its commissioned broker network, which is an expensive way to do business. This system takes away flexibility at a time when discount brokerage and other low-cost distribution methods are gaining market share.

The company has begun installing life insurance specialists in key branches. Merrill has also set up client service departments staffed by salaried employees in 150 branches to screen walk-in traffic and handle small accounts. Merrill had previously attempted to establish a salaried corps of "financial counselor agents" as a wedge that the company could drive between the broker and clients as part of an attempt to gain control of the marketing or distribution function. This would have allowed Merrill Lynch to gain the primary share of the profit derived from a product. However, the effort was disbanded.

Merrill Lynch has a sizable interest in the cable television company Financial News and is participating in two videotex pilot programs. It is also experimenting with a two-way cable system that provides Merrill Lynch's research through Dow Jones News/Retrieval. Merrill also owns a minority interest in Comp-U-Card, which offers a range of merchandise by telephone and by mail. The company is also trying to identify financial products that it could wholesale to department stores without siphoning off business from its own branches. Merrill Lynch is essentially positioning itself to automate the delivery of investment information, should that become necessary. However, to prevent clients from bypassing their brokers, the company is likely to go only as far in widening the distribution of its proprietary data as is required to fend off competition. Merrill does not want to give customers the ability to make investment transactions electronically.

Merrill Lynch may be the best of the large retail brokerage firms. It has certainly been creative and innovative, but competition from Sears, American Express, the banks, and the thrifts, as well as a changing distribution or marketing system, will require more innovation and creativity in the future in order to survive and continue to earn handsome profits.

Sears

Sears is not exactly a newcomer to the financial services industry. The company began providing installment credit on purchases in 1911 (several years before banks authorized similar transactions) and introduced auto insurance in the 1920s. More recently, Sears entered a joint venture with IBM to start a videotex service. It also announced plans in the fourth quarter of 1984 to buy a Delaware bank and convert it to a nonbank bank, which would allow it to sidestep federal restrictions on interstate banking. In addition, Sears is considering issuing a general-purpose credit card that could be competitive with VISA and MasterCard. The card might have the following features: acceptance at a wide range of merchants and department stores (including Sears), hotels, restaurants, oil companies, and supermarkets. Also, the card would offer special low interest rates for major purchases, access to cash nationwide via ATMs, personalized check cashing at Sears stores, travel insurance, and discounts on car rentals.

In a way, Sears, Roebuck is even more of a financial conglomerate than Merrill Lynch. Through Allstate, its property, casualty, and life insurance subsidiary, with 3,250 sales locations; Dean Witter, with almost 600 sales offices and 16,000 employees; Coldwell Banker, with 723 offices and its claim to 4 percent of the nation's residential resale market; the Sears Savings Bank, with almost 100 branches in California and close to $6 billion in deposits at the beginning of 1985; Sears World Trading Company; nearly 4,000 outlets in department stores and catalog offices; a new check processing service to be offered in conjunction with credit unions; and its base of 26 million active credit card holders, Sears may well be a model of future financial conglomerates (see table 4–1).[4]

Sears has launched an array of additional services that include:

The formation of a world trading company in conjunction with the First National Bank of Chicago;

A debit card that could be used to endow the new money market fund accounts with savings and checking account privileges and a universal financial card capable of handling practically all household financial transactions;

Secured and unsecured personal lending including homeowners loans that should rival finance companies, banks, and thrifts;

Two-way communications with the home through computers and telephones for financial and consumer product transactions;

A nationwide linkage of automated teller machines (ATMs) in Sears retail stores that could hook up to bank-like Sears merchandise credit accounts (this would allow customers to draw cash, take small personal loans through prearranged lines of credit, deposit money, or make mer-

Table 4–1
Sears, Roebuck 1983 Revenues and Net Income[a]

| | Revenues | | Net Income[b] | |
	$ billions	Percentage of Total	$ millions	Percentage of Total
Merchandising	$ 25.1	69.6	$ 781	52.6
Allstate Insurance	8.1	22.5	555	37.4
Dean Witter[c]	2.1	6.9	100	6.7
Coldwell Banker	0.7	2.0	48	3.3
	$ 35.9	100.0	$1.34 billion	100.0

[a]It is interesting to note that of Sears's 1978 revenues ($24.4 billion) merchandising contributed 78 percent, Allstate 21 percent, and financial services 1 percent.
[b]This figure is obtained by adding net income column and then subtracting losses of $12 million from the World Trading Company as well as the cost of corporate overhead.
[c]Includes Sears Savings Bank, which contributed revenues of about $430 million and profits of approximately $40 million.

chandise, mortgage, insurance premium, or stock purchase payments); Sears would also have agreements with certain banks so that customers of those banks could use ATMs at Sears stores to tap their savings or checking accounts or even to pay bills;

The sale of conventionally mortgage-backed securities to the public;

A home buying plan through Coldwell Banker that will give some buyers discounts on Sears furniture, appliances, and carpeting;

A revolving credit line backed by home equity that will permit participating homeowners to write checks against their credit lines.

Dean Witter hopes to gain millions of new well-heeled customers from among the customer base at Sears. Sears customers would eventually be able to buy a house, obtain a mortgage, furnish the house, insure it and their own lives, invest idle funds in a high-yield, low-risk money market fund, and buy securities—the ultimate in one-stop shopping. However, retailing and financial services may be difficult to combine, since the businesses have different rhythms, cash needs, and selling methods.[5]

Sears credit card customers will eventually get Dean Witter promotional pieces in their monthly statements. Although mail order marketing has worked for money market funds and some forms of life and health insurance, it has not been successful for many other financial products. For example, Sears has not been particularly successful at selling Allstate auto insurance through Sears catalogs.[6]

Sears has opened financial service centers in stores in major metropolitan areas and plans to have about 600 centers by the end of 1986. These financial service centers are located in high-traffic areas of the stores where Sears hopes to lure shoppers to sell them insurance, IRAs, stocks, bonds, and real estate. Sears strategy is based on generating the same lifelong customer loyalty for its financial services that they have earned for their tools and appliances. The success of Sears's strategy depends on whether its traditional customers need and will actually use the Sears financial centers. The company's 859 stores could double as full-scale financial service centers, but there is a question as to whether there are enough upper-income individuals frequenting the stores to make it worthwhile.

Interactive television could be the vehicle that integrates the entire retail distribution system: stores, catalogs, and insurance and brokerage offices. Although the potential for cross-selling and the introduction of these new products seem promising, there are some pitfalls to be avoided. As the company pushes more direct selling of merchandise and finances, notably through interactive television and home computer systems, it may steal sales from its own stores. Retail discount stores are already a threat on the merchandise front, while discount brokers represent a real threat on the retail brokerage front. Equally alarming, direct selling via television or through the mailman bypasses its large commissioned network at Dean Witter and Allstate. Another potential problem is that by becoming a competitor in real estate through Coldwell Banker, Sears may lose current business with other financial institutions such as the property insurance referrals Allstate gets from real estate brokers.

Sears and First Chicago joined forces in 1983 to set up a major world trading company under the Bank Export Services Act of 1982. Sears World Trade expects to become the world's largest general trading company. The joint venture will help develop the Sears world trade network and provide the banking arm for the trading company. The Sears arm of the venture will perform product and market research, and acquire and move the goods, while First Chicago will finance both ends of the trade. Through the joint venture, First Chicago will be able to reach thousands of so-called middle-market companies throughout the United States and help them not only develop exports but finance the trade as well. The problem with this strategy is that the world may not need any more trading companies. Even the Japanese trading companies are beginning to suffer from the lack of business as former customers make other arrangements.

Sears provides lockbox services for Mellon Bank in Atlanta, Boston, Los Angeles, Philadelphia, Columbus, and Jacksonville. The arrangement enables Sears to utilize excess processing capacity and Mellon to become one of the few banks offering interstate lockbox services. The lockbox reduces mail float for the bank's corporate customers, and decreases processing costs, since many of the checks received could be processed locally and not as interregional items through the Federal Reserve's check processing system.

Sears has also reached an agreement to process credit card transactions for some Phillips Petroleum Company service stations. Sears plans to begin with a test involving twenty-eight Phillips service stations and twelve Sears stores in Oklahoma. Sears computers will provide credit authorization and recording of credit card transactions and will transmit them to Phillips's credit card center. Sears also processes retail remittances for certain customers at Mellon Bank. Sears intends to use its computer and communication systems to offer bill-processing services to other concerns. In addition, Sears has reached an agreement with MCI Communication Corporation to test market a telephone bill payment service in southern California.

Sears Mortgage Security Corp. has begun to buy mortgages in order to resell them as securities in the secondary market. They join private-sector companies such as Residential Funding Corp. (a subsidiary of Norwest Corp.) and General Electric Mortgage Securities Corp. (a subsidiary of GECC), as well as government agencies such as the Federal Home Loan Mortgage Corp. and the Federal National Mortgage Association. The market for the private conduits is primarily with loans in excess of $115,300, the limit that Congress has placed on mortgage loans by the aforementioned government agencies.

American Express

American Express Company faces a huge challenge in successfully integrating the securities firms of Shearson Loeb Rhoades, Lehman, Foster and Marshall, and Robinson-Humphrey into its financial empire. It also must integrate Investors Diversified Services (IDS). Of course, American Express is best known for its travel service and credit card business. Its major assets include a large international bank, Warner Amex Cable Communications, Fireman's Fund Insurance, Mitchell Beazly (a publishing company), and a modest interest in McLeon Young Weir (a major Canadian securities firm).

American Express is moving beyond travel and leisure dollars to vie for its share of the retail financial services marketplace. The company is counting on two aspects of its business to help it do so: (1) its reach into the affluent sector of the economy through its 14 million cardholders, whom it views as nearly recession-proof and (2) its data processing ability and information systems. American Express wishes to become an omnipresent intermediary for affluent Americans, tapping into the estimated $9 trillion of personal assets in the United States.[7] American Express is now the nation's largest manager of other people's money, with approximately $44 billion under management.

Competition for upscale consumers of financial services is intense because most companies are targeting the same market. Many observers feel that American Express is better tapped into the "cult of affluence" than is the competition. One reason for this is the belief that American Express card holders (on average) have 2.5 times the net worth of those without a card.

American Express has acquired the foreign banking network of Geneva-based Trade Development Bank Holding, S.A., the fifth-largest Swiss bank. The acquisition was merged into American Express International Banking Corporation. The sale excluded Trade Development's 61 percent holding of Republic New York Corporation. Current banking laws prohibit American Express, which owns a securities firm and an insurance company, from owning a U.S. bank.

The combination promises American Express an expanded base of wealthy foreign customers in addition to its 14 million charge-card holders and its investment and insurance clients. These new foreign banking customers represent a potentially lucrative market for investment products in real estate, securities, and oil and gas drilling limited partnerships sold by American Express. Also, these clients are unlikely to be stolen away by the rapidly growing discount brokers. Personal banking assets under management rose to $6 billion from $1.5 billion prior to the merger, while total assets reached $13.1 billion, up from $7.8 billion.

American Express has expanded its ATM service to more regions of the country in an effort to capture a larger share of the credit card market. It should be mentioned, however, that any national or even international network of ATMs could lead to less use of American Express travelers' checks. The Express Cash system allows card holders to draw up to $500 a week from twenty-four-hour cash machines at over 1,200 locations throughout the country for a $1.00 fee per transaction. Close to 300 of these machines are installed in Publix Super Markets in Florida in an agreement reached with Sun Banks of Florida. The system also includes close to 100 American Express travelers' check machines, which provide card holders with travelers' checks at hotels and airports. At this writing, the company was planning to install some travelers' check machines in Europe and was exploring the possibility of affiliating its Express Cash network with European banks. American Express does not view ATMs as a profit-making endeavor. The goal is market penetration and use of the card, not per-unit profit, according to Herbert E. Goodfriend, Prudential-Bache Securities analyst.

In addition to its credit card base of customers, American Express can also reach affluent Americans through more than 5,500 brokers in its system. According to Sanford I. Weil, American Express president, these sources provide "the ultimate link with the high-net-worth individual." Some experts believe that American Express data processing and communications expertise gives them a leg up on Wall Street rivals. James D. Robinson III, Amerian Express Company's chairman, has always considered "the effective delivery of information" a central aspect of every business that the company has entered.

Warner Amex Cable constructs and operates cable systems that provide video programming and other services to residential and commercial subscribers often via satellite networks. When all the systems are fully operational, the cable system, with franchises in Dallas, Houston, Pittsburgh, Cincinnati, Columbus, suburban Chicago, St. Louis, and sections of New York City, should give American Express an entry into many homes and companies. Experiments on providing subscribers with a wealth of information from data banks, such as the *New York Times*, the *Washington Post*, and the Associated Press, are being conducted in a joint effort between Warner Amex, Atari, and Compuserve.

The tie-in with Warner Amex Cable Communications could put American Express in the forefront of electronic consumer financial transactions on cable television screens. The company is exploring other sophisticated interactive home services such as electronic banking and shopping and commercial services for business. Personal lines insurance and travel arrangements should eventually be available from either the home computer or cable television screens. It also should be possible to have either an airline ticket or an insurance policy printed instantly and made immediately available. The cable TV system may also have a slot where viewers can insert an American Express card for payment.[8]

Shearson/American Express also owns Balcor Company, a fast-growing major real estate syndicator. In addition to packaging real estate investments for brokerage investors, Balcor will develop products for overseas clients of American Express International Banking Corporation and for customers of Fireman's Fund Insurance.

Shearson/American Express has developed a computerized cash management service called the Financial Management Account (FMA), which is similar to the CMA established by Merrill Lynch. Since FMA customers will use an American Express Gold Card in conjunction with their account when they make a purchase, American Express will receive a discount from the merchant because its card is used.

American Express has acquired the Minneapolis-based Investors Diversified Services Unit (IDS), which manages fourteen mutual funds, markets insurance and annuities, and manages pension funds. This purchase has given Amex a large foothold in mutual funds, where IDS has more than $8.8 billion under management, as well as the company's $17.5 billion in assets under management. It has also given Amex new insurance products such as annuities and term life insurance. IDS has $13.5 billion of life insurance in force.

The acquisitions of Shearson and the Trade Development Bank were designed to gain a foothold in the top end of the market for the high net worth individual. However, IDS has a huge door-to-door sales force of 4,500, which has given Amex direct access to the mass middle-market in the United States, where IDS has 1.1 million customers—the home turf of Sears, Prudential, and the banks. The decision by Shearson to buy IDS was originally linked to an unsuccessful direct-mail campaign to interest Amex cardholders in IRAs and other investments. According to Weil, president of Amex, "you can get people interested through direct mail, but in order to get people to do something, someone has to make contact."

IDS also presents a set of mutual fund accounts into which Shearson can sweep brokerage accounts. American Express credit card customers will be able to withdraw these funds or make deposits into them via ATM machines. The strategy could be one of "tied-sales" rather than cross-selling. If an individual desires X, he or she must have Y.

Although American Express is likely to face continuing earnings problems in two subsidiaries—Fireman's Fund and Warner Amex Cable Communications—so far they have been able for the most part to integrate their acquisitions rather successfully while still maintaining a strong balance sheet. Weil and Cohen have been able to generate cost savings in most of their brokerage operations. They have been able to add revenues and judiciously control costs, particularly in back-room operations and other areas of duplication of effort.

However, Wall Street analysts were unhappy with the company's first decline in profits in thirty-five years. Some analysts have voiced concern that American Express has acquired so many companies so quickly that it risks losing control over some of them and not integrating them properly.

On the other hand, supporters of the company point out that the cash flows and borrowing needs of the various subsidiaries are coordinated by the company's treasurer in New York, helping to reduce outside borrowing. Also, they cite several examples of one subsidiary selling products or services of another, including the following:

1. Flight insurance and travel insurance for American Express card holders are underwritten by Fireman's Fund;
2. American Express credit card holders are offered term life insurance through mailings;
3. Shearson offers a brokerage account hooked up to an American Express Gold Card;
4. Investment bankers at Shearson Lehman have arranged several loans for clients through American Express International Banking Corp.

Shearson/American Express agreed in April 1984 to acquire Lehman Brothers Kuhn Loeb for a combined package of convertible debt and subordinated notes valued at $360 million in subordinated debt of Lehman. The combined firm would be called Shearson/American Express.

The purchase gives Shearson and its parent American Express Company a primary dealership in U.S. government securities, as well as a strong investment banking and fixed income and equity trading units, weak areas at Shearson. The combined firm would have the second-largest capital position behind Merrill Lynch and hold the number six position in underwriting as lead manager (see table 4–2).

The most dramatic benefits have probably come from linking the names of Shearson, Lehman, and IDS with American Express, one of the best-known

Table 4–2
Lehman and Shearson/American Express, 1983

	Shearson	*Lehman*	*Combined*
Net income	$175 million	$60 million	$235 million
Number of employees	13,465	2,906	16,371
Number of registered representatives	4,758	495	5,253
Number of offices	364	11	375

and -respected brand names in the world. According to Louis V. Gerstan, Jr., the chairman of the traveler's related service unit, "There's a great cacaphony in the market place today. . . . Everyone's screaming about how his IRA . . . or personal financial adviser is the best. The winners are going to be people who established a clear consumer franchise that stands for something."

Citicorp

Citicorp is a global financial services enterprise and information company with the United States as its home base. At the end of 1983 Citicorp had assets of approximately $135 billion, which at that time made them the largest bank holding company in the United States. Walter Wriston, the former chairman of Citicorp, described Citicorp as one of a handful of financial supermarkets that will be able to handle virtually any transaction. These financial conglomerates, communicating with customers via home computers, will allow the customer to bank at home, buy stocks, bonds, and insurance, obtain theater listings, buy airline tickets, and even shop for food, clothing, and appliances at the lowest possible prices without leaving home. The customer will even be able to pay for these goods and services with a credit card issued by the financial conglomerate.

Technological Orientation

Citicorp is a pioneer in ATMs and in interactive home computers. The bank holding company can compete with commercial companies in data processing and communications. The company also expects to satisfy customer information needs such as financial and credit information, economic, business, and financial news, as well as industry and country trends. Citicorp even runs a small hotel and convention center in suburban New York City, publishes books on banking, and sells publications produced by its economics department.

The company has designed and produced its own internal telephone system and laid its own fiber-optic transmission cables under the streets of New York City in an attempt to make the bank independent of common carriers. Citicorp has also purchased its own transporter on a space satellite and has applied to the FCC for licenses for microwave broadcasting in more than a dozen metropolitan areas around the country.

With the slogan "The Citi Never Sleeps" the bank is a major believer in the plastic card. It owns Diner's Club and Carte Blanche travel and expense cards and offers its own MasterCard and VISA credit cards throughout the country. As a matter of fact, Citicorp is the nation's largest bank-card issuer, with about 12 million accounts. The company is also the developer of private-label credit cards for merchants such as Goodyear and Tandy Radio Shack. It also has the Citibank card, which enables customers to use the bank's ATMs. The bank envisions a single plastic card that embodies the financial potential of all the aforementioned cards plus that of a debit card that can be used anywhere in the country.

Citicorp has developed Home Base, a system that allows customers to do more of their financial chores from home. They can open additional accounts, update existing accounts and credit-card balances, pay bills, and keep up on financial news. However, they must still leave their home to make a deposit unless they choose to make the deposit by mail. A Home Base customer is linked to the bank by a combination of personal computers and television sets for a $10 monthly service fee.

Traditional thin-spread institutional lending has become anachronistic at Citibank. The compensating balances of yesterday, which made base-rate lending profitable, are fading away. Citicorp recognizes that if they are not being compensated via fees for services, they may not be compensated at all. Essentially, asset growth on the books of Citicorp is being discouraged, and the holding company is concentrating on pass-throughs and fee generation. However, the company recognizes that it must have both the asset-generating capability and the distribution capability to operate in this vein. For example, Citicorp has upgraded the commodity loan into a proprietary service package and enjoys fees for this package.

Citicorp has acquired a tiny bank in South Dakota as a way to enter the insurance business. The theory is that Citicorp, by doing its insurance business through a state-chartered bank, would be able to circumvent the 1982 federal law that specifically prohibits bank holding companies from engaging in most facets of insurance. The bold and innovative back-door approach is vintage Citicorp. For decades, Citicorp has been trying to strip away the layers of federal regulations.

However, at the request of the Federal Reserve Board, the bank temporarily withdrew its application to sell insurance out of South Dakota. The regulatory body indicated that banking's entry into insurance should be addressed at a national level by Congress, and so the South Dakota connection has been at least temporarily stalled. However, Citibank has joined a growing number of banks that provide branch space for financial services that they are not permitted to sell directly. Citibank has begun offering life insurance policies at select branches through AIG. Citibank receives a flat rate or percentage of sales, whichever is higher, for the use of the space for the sale of term, universal life, and whole life policies. Citibank also intends to offer insurance policies for car owners, homeowners, and renters. Separately, Citibank makes life and health insurance available to its MasterCard and VISA card holders under another arrangement with insurance companies.

The Garn–St. Germain Act outlaws property and casualty insurance opportunities for bank holding companies. However, Citicorp has a homeowners property and casualty business operation through seventeen agencies across the country, and some of their programs have been grandfathered. They offer homeowners insurance out of several vehicles including agencies in Arizona, California, and Missouri. Citicorp expects greater insurance sales from their mortgage customers by offering creative insurance products covering the balances on Citibank private-label credit cards.

Citicorp wants to engage in all forms of life underwriting and will offer the more conservative end of the property casualty spectrum—for example, insurance for cars, recreational vehicles, houses, and mobile homes, as well as title insurance. Citicorp will initially engage in insurance distribution, as opposed to underwriting, until the legal barriers fall in the United States. Citicorp can be expected eventually to become an underwriter for target markets focusing on financial guarantees and the funds flow side of the business, since the skills required are really banking skills.

Citicorp feels that it can deliver standard insurance policies, such as term life coverage, homeowner's, and automobile, for a total administrative and agent expense of about 15 cents of the premium dollar compared to 25 to 30 cents that are now spent by insurance companies. This would be accomplished by reducing the agent's commission, which now averages 15 cents of the premium delivery, by developing an efficient and increasingly cost-effective distribution system. Citicorp would sell insurance to its credit cardholders—one of every twelve households within the United States—and at national savings and loans and industrial banks that it has acquired in states such as California, Illinois, and Florida. A Citicorp belief that insurance and banking are functionally similar lies behind their application to acquire a state-chartered bank in South Dakota, where a bank can sell insurance. Although the application has been deferred by the Federal Reserve Board pending further consideration by Congress on the issues raised by expanded bank holding company powers, the Fed did approve Citicorp's application to engage in unrestricted life insurance underwriting in the United Kingdom.

Walter Wriston has provided a succinct statement of the Citibank view of regulation: "The solution is not to take away the freedoms that make our non-banking competition more vigorous. It is to let us compete under regulations framed . . . on the real world . . . [and] to give us the flexibility to provide that competition which always improves services to the public."[9]

Citicorp was innovative in its purchase of a failing $3 billion California thrift institution in 1982 and other failing thrifts in Illinois and Florida. This has given Citicorp a retail foothold in California and Florida. Citicorp has also purchased a failing commercial bank in Puerto Rico.

Citicorp has left no doubt about its interest in the lucrative southern California market. The company has converted its sixteen Person-to-Person

Financial Centers (which offer consumer loans) into branches of its Oakland-headquartered savings and loan. Citicorp has also announced plans to build a forty-two-story office tower in the financial district of Los Angeles.

In a *New York Times Magazine* interview (published on May 29, 1983), Wriston turned from talk of technology and expansion to speak of banking basics: "The nuts and bolts of lending money is getting it back. . . . That still depends upon human judgments." Citibank is one of the premier international lending banks in the country with international loans equaling more than 60 percent of the total loan portfolio. International loans are not without their problems. For example, Citicorp has in excess of $40 billion of dollar-denominated loans to Brazil, which, like many of its Latin American neighbors, is having difficulty meeting its payments.

Citicorp also has 229 consumer finance and mortgage lending offices in fifty-five cities. If loan production and Edge Act offices are included they have 400 domestic offices compared to 200 offices at MHC in 1983. In addition Citicorp has close to 300 New York City area branches, Citicorp Services (travel services and travelers checks), Advance Mortgage (mortgages and mobile homes), Citibank International and Citibank Overseas Investment (Edge Act Office), Nationwide Financial Service (consumer finance with 171 offices in twenty-four states), Citicorp Commercial (business financing), Citicorp Business Credit (commercial finance, factoring), Citicorp Leasing (equipment leasing), and Citibank Delaware.

On the international front Citibank has over 200 branches in almost 100 countries. The company has 2,400 offices in ninety-four countries abroad. In 1982 international operations accounted for 61 percent of income. Citicorp has extensive consumer financial operations in Great Britain, France, Belgium, West Germany, Hong Kong, and Australia, as well as investment or merchant banking operations in West Germany and London.

In early February 1984 the Federal Reserve Board approved a request by Citicorp to set up subsidiaries in Kentucky and Tennessee to engage in industrial banking. The bank would offer consumer and commercial loans and accept time and savings deposits. The holding company is expected to set up similar subsidiaries at key locations across the country.

In the same month Citicorp gained the Comptroller of the Currency's approval to set up a banking operation in Maine. The move would make New York-based Citicorp the first federally chartered out-of-state bank to set up operations in Maine, which passed a law in 1975 permitting entry there by bank holding companies from other states, if those states allow Maine banks to operate within their borders.

Citicorp still needs approval of the move from the Federal Reserve Board, which regulates bank holding companies. The company's action reflects a sharp increase in banking activity across state lines despite federal laws against interstate banking. In addition to allowing reciprocal arrangements with other states, some states allow outside banks to set up limited operations without reciprocity.

Citicorp does some business in forty states and the District of Columbia. The expansion not only adds to the company's reach nationwide, it also increases pressure on Congress to enact general federal legislation liberalizing bank activities. In another related move New Mexico legislators rejected Citicorp's bid to open a bank in Santa Fe. Citicorp wanted to open a regional credit card processing center in New Mexico similar to its operation in South Dakota. With a national bank charter, Citicorp said it could export New Mexico's unrestricted interest rates to other southwestern and Rocky Mountain states. When Citicorp made Nevada the same offer it posed in New Mexico, the offer was accepted.

Citicorp took a major step toward becoming a global stockbroker when it announced its plan in November 1983 to buy a 29.9 percent (the maximum holding foreigners are allowed) interest in Vickers da Costa PLC, a British brokerage firm. In addition, Citicorp would acquire majority ownership of Vickers da Costa's overseas offices in Hong Kong, Singapore, Tokyo, and New York. The purchase, which would be made by Citicorp's Capital Markets Group, "fits in with Citicorp's efforts to build an investment-banking business in countries where it is permitted." In addition, the brokerage firm's list of affluent clients could prove lucrative for Citicorp to court with other financial services.

Citicorp has joined forces with leading supermarkets in Florida (Publix Super Markets, Inc.) and California (Safeway Stores, Inc.) to give its credit card holders easy access to cash. The giant bank holding company expects to reach similar accords in the New York–Connecticut–New Jersey region. The move into supermarkets is viewed by some banking analysts as a step in Citicorp's effort to provide a full range of banking services to customers throughout the country. Unlike accords in which banks in different parts of the country have agreed to share ATMs for the convenience of travelers, Citicorp's strategy is to develop a comprehensive consumer banking business in local areas nationwide: Citicorp's move could speed the process toward interstate banking and could increase pressure on banks that operate large and costly branch systems. A bank that can deliver banking services more cheaply by using machines, telephones, and the mail can present formidable competition to banks still operating expensive branch networks. Through credit and debit cards, mail service, and toll-free telephone numbers, Citicorp already offers its customers just about any banking service. Citibank has begun marketing a "Citibank financial account" combining a credit card, savings, checking, a credit line, and other features in three initial metropolitan areas: Atlanta, Tampa, and Minneapolis–St. Paul.

Citibank has begun to market FOCUS, its CMA look-alike. The company has had some difficulty in marketing the service and has signed an agreement with CIGNA Corp. to offer FOCUS through its independent agents in the New York area.

The company's consumer banking business, after a multiyear period of un-profitability, is now in the black. Citicorp had a $29 billion consumer loan port-folio in early 1984, which, if analyzed separately, would be the twelfth-largest bank in the United States. The company envisions a world of 35 million Citicorp customers producing earnings of $30 per customer. Citibank invested heavily in electronic banking systems and is the industry's low-cost producer. This gives Citicorp the flexibility to pay more for deposits and gain market share or, alter-natively, to meet the market rate and generate above-average profit margins.

While Citicorp earned $723 million in 1982, the Capital Markets Group contributed $100 million of after-tax income. The Capital Markets Group posted a 1.20 percent return on assets (ROA) and a return on equity (ROE) of 30 percent, approximately twice Citicorp's ROA of 0.61 percent and ROE of 16.4 percent. Citicorp conducts perhaps the premier investment banking activity among bank holding companies. Citicorp makes the case to its cor-porate clients that its breadth of international activities allows it to raise funds outside of the United States at a cost comparable to domestic financing. Citibank is also among the top institutions in merger and acquisition activity.

With major corporations satisfying much of their funding needs with commercial paper rather than through bank loans, and with foreign banks muscling into the U.S. corporate loan market, domestic banks, such as Citi-bank, are developing a large appetite for the capital markets' high-margin, fee-based business.

Citibank has one of the largest trust departments among banks in the United States. The trust department is a major manager of pension and profit sharing plans, individual trust accounts, and foreign and local governmental funds.

Expanding its activities in the securities business, Citibank began offering discount brokerage services at its 275 branches in the New York City area. To open a brokerage account customers are required to deposit at least $2,500 in an insured market rate account. The accounts are handled by Q & R Clearing Corp., a unit of Quick & Reilly. Dividends and interest paid into the accounts are swept into the market account on a daily basis. The bank plans to install special brokerage kiosks, as well as stock quotation terminals, at a number of branches. The transactions will be handled by bank personnel who have been trained to handle securities transactions. The dis-count brokerage account appeals to people who do not have a brokerage ac-count as well as customers who wish to save 40 to 70 percent off the rate charged by nondiscount brokers. Citibank also offers brokerage services as part of its "personal assets account," including money funds, credit, and a range of banking and investment services, for a yearly fee.

Manufacturers Hanover Corporation (MHC)

Manufacturers Hanover Corporation is a financial services organization that has been transformed from a single bank in a single city with only a limited presence abroad into an organization with close to 1,100 offices throughout the United States and 103 facilities in forty-one countries. The primary holding of Manufacturers Hanover Corporation is Manufacturers Hanover Trust Co. (MHT), the fourth-largest bank in the United States with headquarters in New York City. "Manny Hanny," as it is affectionately called, has lived in the shadow of New York competitors Citicorp and J.P. Morgan, which, according to a *Wall Street Journal* front page article, have historically been more imaginative and innovative and certainly more conscious of increased public relations pizazz. On the other hand, despite its lack of pizazz, Manny Hanny is a highly respected institution with an aggressive lending posture, the lowest ratio of nonperforming to total loans of any large New York bank (prior to its Latin American loan problems), and an exceptionally strong correspondent banking network. As a matter of fact, MHC had eleven consecutive years of record earnings with a compound annual rate of earnings growth in the five-year period ending 1983 of 13.4 percent. Senior management is intelligent and hard working, while the banking atmosphere is harmonious and tension free (see table 4–3).

Manufacturers Hanover Commercial Corporation is an industry leader in two lines of business: factoring and commercial finance. Manufacturers Hanover Leasing Corporation is the largest bank-affiliated leasing and equipment finance company in the nation, with a managed and direct portfolio of $5 billion based on original equipment cost.

The International Division covers virtually all corners of the globe through an extensive network of twenty-two branches, thirty representative offices, eight subsidiaries, and affiliates in forty-one countries. In addition, MHT has seven Edge Act offices in the United States. During 1983 foreign operations accounted for 49 percent of the corporation's net income, while foreign assets represented 47.2 percent of the average total assets. MHT has established regional processing centers in Hong Kong, Singapore, and Bahrain to provide on-the-spot data capture capability and interaction with customers in their own time zones and in their own language. This should reduce communications costs, improve efficiency, and speed up the operations process.

The North American Division incorporates lending and corresponding banking in the United States and Canada. A Special Finance Division was also established to draw together the complex pieces of venture capital, commercial finance, leasing, and unsecured credit. The division places into one unit the considerable expertise in financing acquisitions, mergers, spin-offs, and the movement of companies into or out of the public markets. An energy division was also formed to deal with the growth of energy-related financing worldwide.

The Retail Banking Group includes the New York City branch system, the upstate bank, and nationwide network of finance offices. The basic goals of the division are to build up credit outstandings and cost-effective deposit volumes, to generate fee income, and to control the expense base. The retail network has 270 branches in New York and has 379 national facilities that

Table 4–3
Manufacturers Hanover Trust versus the Competition

	Annualized Return on Assets	Return on Equity	Net Interest Margin	Long-Term Debt/Capital	Nonperforming Assets/Loans and OREO
Manufacturers Hanover Corp.	0.55%	13.42%	3.23%	47.81%	1.95%
Bankers Trust New York Corp.	0.71%	15.69%	3.03%	19.06%	2.61%
Chase Manhattan Corp.	0.54%	13.11%	3.49%	27.78%	3.52%
Citicorp	0.61%	16.47%	3.90%	67.72%	2.42%
J.P. Morgan Co.	0.88%	15.29%	3.00%	19.29%	1.88%

Sources: Cates Consulting Analysts, Keefe Bruyette & Woods, Goldman Sachs Fixed Income Research.

Note: Figures based on year end 1983.

range from large core offices specializing in home equity loans, sales finance, and vendor programs to smaller shopping center–type offices aimed at the retail trade. Branches are being consolidated where they are not profitable, shrunk in size, and better automated.

Manny Hanny provides a full range of banking services to the real estate industry nationwide. Primary emphasis is on developing and expanding relationships with major owners, developers, and investors. It provides credit and noncredit services, investment advisory services, and a supporting arm to the branch systems' residential mortgage lending programs. MH Mortgage Corporation is one of the nation's largest mortgage bankers, with products and services that include residential mortgages, residential and commercial construction financing, as well as permanent mortgage financing for commercial projects. The company manages a $7 billion mortgage servicing portfolio and is active in the marketing of residential loans in the secondary market and of commercial real estate loans in the private placement market.

The Portfolio and Investment Banking Division handles a broad spectrum of investment banking and funding activities for MHC, including dealer operations in U.S. government and municipal securities and money market instruments, public finance, and asset and liability management. The division operates six representative offices in the United States and a subsidiary company based in Wilmington, Delaware.

The Trust Division was unbundled into its functional parts. Manufacturers Hanover Investment Corporation, a separate investment management subsidiary with more than $24 billion in assets under management, was formed to serve the pension fund market. The unbundling of the trust department entailed the creation of an Institutional Trust and Agency Division, better known as the Corporate Trust Division. MHT's goal is to become the industry leader in this area. The final piece resulting from the unbundling of the Trust Division was the private Banking and Securities Industry Division. MHT has married the standard lending tools to its trust operation to assist in the creation of wealth as well as the management of wealth. The Wall Street Department, a premier lender to the securities industry, is also part of this newly formed division.

At the time of this writing, MHT did not have a discount brokerage operation, sell insurance other than credit insurance, or own a savings and loan. However, it did own a small industrial bank in Colorado and a small thrift and loan in California.

MHC made the largest acquisition by a bank holding company when it purchased C.I.T. Financial Corporation for $1.5 billion from RCA. C.I.T. is a major provider of financing to medium-size business for inventories, aircraft, construction, medical and energy equipment, machine tools, and factoring services. Menhard Commercial Corporation and William Iselin and Company, C.I.T. subsidiaries, are well-known nationwide factoring companies. C.I.T. also has a major leasing division as well as a consumer lending arm that concentrates principally on mobile home loans and second mortgages.

The acquisition should enable Manufacturers Hanover to generate quality domestic assets with above-average yields. The acquisition appears to be a logical extension of the MHC game plan to gain a nationwide presence in local and consumer markets that cannot be served long-distance out of New York. With the acquisition MHC will have offices in forty-four states. This may not be interstate banking in the traditional sense, but it is interstate banking in the real sense. C.I.T.'s corporate lending base of middle-size companies complements those of MHT, which primarily deals with larger corporations. With the acquisition of C.I.T., Manufacturers Hanover Corporation's nonbank subsidiaries will account for 20 percent of its earnings. Combined earnings of more than $180 million came from the nonbank subsidiaries of MHC in 1984.

MHC believes that the national middle-market offers some of the best combinations of good growth and high margins and that corporate subsidiaries should generate a return on assets higher than that of the flagship bank. For example, the return on assets (ROA) of C.I.T. is 1.8 percent, which is considerably higher than the returns available in banking. As a matter of fact, C.I.T.'s ROA is some 80 to 90 basis points better than even the ROA of the most highly regarded regional banks and approximately 3 times the ROA at the flagship bank. Since MHC would have a combined earnings power of $180 million from its nonbank subsidiaries, it is able to set a goal of 1.0 for its ROA, up from a current level of 0.60.

The real question that must be answered is whether the C.I.T. acquisition will really be beneficial to the company. The acquisition appears strategically sound in the long run, but in the short-run the costly C.I.T. purchase has forced the bank to issue more stock, dilute its near-term earnings per-share, weaken the balance sheet, and reduce the flexibility to make future acquisitions.

C.I.T. also provides diversification into new businesses and geographic markets. Most of the C.I.T. loans are to small and medium-size corporations. These smaller companies usually do not have alternative sources of financing, such as selling commercial paper, that are available to larger companies. Therefore, profit margins are considerably wider. MHT's leasing operations have focused on high-priced items such as airplanes, ships, and railroad rolling stock, while C.I.T. is strong in industrial financing for such things as machine tools, construction equipment, and hospital apparatus. MHT also coveted C.I.T.'s big role in mobile-home financing and consumer lending, which reach a more affluent market than the bank's own consumer-finance operation. Another big prize is C.I.T.'s nationwide network of more than 350 offices, to be added to Manufacturers' 740 offices. The move essentially makes MHT a bank with branches all over the country. When interstate banking occurs, the bank should be able to set up a drive-in window or a counter for cashiers to transact retail business.

In proportion to capital, Manufacturers' Latin American exposure and standby letters of credit outstanding are the highest of any U.S. bank. While the bank increased its reserves substantially for possible loan losses in 1983, that cushion still is small beside the reserves of many competitors. Low bank reserves can prop up earnings, but if the loans turn sour, MHT would take a harder hit than other banks.

Historically, MHT tended to open representative offices rather than establish branches abroad on the international front. This strategy offers both pluses and minuses. On the plus side it enabled the bank to win many correspondent friends because the bank did not battle head to head against local banks. It concentrated on offering such services as trade finance and dollar settlements to local banks. It is estimated that somewhere between 25 and 35 percent of MHT's operating earnings come from foreign correspondent banks. On the negative side is the lack of full-service branches without local deposit bases from which to make local currency loans, especially in Latin America. Instead, the bank has had to rely on dollar loans, and so its vulnerability to foreign-exchange shortages in countries is greater.

The bank's emphasis on lending volume also should be hurt by the regulatory authorities' suggested increase in minimum capital standards related to assets. This places a premium on loan margins and a penalty on volume. Compounding such problems is the fact that the growth in international lending has slowed, while greater competition from regional and foreign banks has shaved bank profit margins on loans to the biggest U.S. corporations.

Although the bank was slow in introducing automated teller networks, updating its computer and technological capability and in developing meaningful bond and foreign exchange trading operations, Manny Hanny devoted a great deal of catch-up spending to achieving a degree of excellence. Interplex, the cash-management system, is one of the best in banking, and Geonet, the private telecommunications network, provides the bank with a truly global telecommunications system. In its 1982 annual report, MHC stated that "we are committed to even further change—in size and scope, in geographic reach and range of services—but we are also committed to maintaining those values that have always been at the core of our organization: Quality, Loyalty, Consistency. Some things should not change."

General Electric Credit Corporation (GECC)

General Electric Corporation is the country's third-largest finance company in lending volume, ranking behind the consumer-oriented captives of GM and Ford. GE products now account for less than 5 percent of the credit companies' volume, a switch from the 1930s when GECC existed only to serve GE and its customers. GECC has become a large source of commercial and industrial financing, transforming itself into a sophisticated lender resembling a wholesale banker specializing in asset-based financing. In addition, it has 300 branches across the nation, staffed with specialists who have the freedom to structure loans, as long as they are profitable.

The company has reduced its exposure to the less-lucrative consumer finance field. Fixed rates, usury ceilings, increased origination and service costs, higher loan losses, more liberal personal bankruptcy laws, and tougher competition have made the consumer lending business less attractive. The consumer-related financing still runs the gamut from installment sales programs and inventory financing for retailers, to issuing and servicing private label credit cards for department stores, as well as managing receivables for small personal loan companies. GECC has even eased its way out of the retail side of the second mortgage business, shifting to servicing mortgage portfolios of institutions such as Bache-Prudential and Merrill Lynch.

At GECC a corporate customer can borrow to help erect or equip an entire plant, consummate a merger, develop a real estate project, or even drill for oil and gas. The finance company is making medium-term loans in a fashion similar to commercial banks, but it also has the added flexibility of taking part of its return as equity, a practice denied to commercial banks.

GECC is also involved in real estate finance and insurance. It specializes in intermediate-term construction loans. In addition, it develops office building and rental apartment projects, offers wrap-around mortgages and condo conversions.

Interest rates charged by GECC are often below bank rates because:

1. GECC charges no compensating balances;
2. GECC, a AAA credit in the bond market, with an A_1/P_1 commercial paper rating, has a lower cost of commercial paper and long-term debt than most banks;
3. GECC has a favorable tax treatment because of depreciation, ITC, and energy credits, which help shield most of the parent company's pretax profit.

The parent company, General Electric Corporation, believes that GECC's participation in the trillion-dollar financial services industry represents a recessionary and inflation resistant contribution to GE's diversified earnings base. GECC is expected to move more deeply into investment banking and insurance. The latter effort will be pursued via Puritan Insurance Company and Employers Reinsurance Corp., as well as by a partial ownership in FGIC, a company that insures bond issues.

GECC already arranges loan syndications for regular customers and is investigating the possibility of becoming a broker-dealer in larger syndications where many more investors are involved. Its insurance subsidiaries sell GECC-oriented products such as insurance on the cars leased from GECC and travel, accident, and life coverage. It has more recently set up an investment banking business called GEVES, which is a registered broker-dealer. The firm offers a wide variety of investment banking services, especially as they relate to the needs of GECC's commercial finance clients. These include project finance syndicated private placements of debt, equity offerings, and merger and acquisition activity. Another part of its investment banking thrust will be in hedging and arbitrage.

GECC is an extremely profitable and innovative financial services company. It has a return on equity in excess of 13 percent and maintains a seven-to-one ratio of debt to equity, compared with banks, where a twenty-to-one ratio is not uncommon. GECC has been a major competitor of commercial banks in all forms of corporate lending, especially in equipment financing. Leases represent half of GECC's portfolio of earning assets.

GECC has operated as a separate subsidiary of GE Corp. and contributed about 13 percent of the parent's earnings. In the period from 1978 to 1983, GECC's net income has grown an average of 38 percent per year.

Prudential

Prudential, the insurance giant, purchased Bache Halsey Stuart and several regional brokerage firms such as Elkins Co. (Philadelphia), Bruns, Nordeman Reel and Bateman Eichler, and Hill Richards (Los Angeles) in a move viewed as an attempt to gain access to higher-income clientele of the brokerage firms. Both Prudential and Bache have improved cross-selling opportunities in which to offer their financial products and services. George L. Ball, the chief executive officer of Prudential-Bache Securities, has hired well-known securities analysts in the hope that a prestigious Prudential-Bache research group will become the firm's big lure in attracting more commission income by supplying investment recommendations to institutional and individual investors. The company began a cash management service in spring 1982 that is similar to Merrill Lynch's highly successful Cash Management Account. The Bache Command Account combines the high-interest income of a money market fund with the convenience of check writing and credit card withdrawals. In addition to the typical service available in such an account, the investor will have access to Citicorp's Pass Word Service traveler's checks (which can be ordered by telephone and delivered) and have access to Comp-U-Card, a national computerized shopping service. Purchases made on a VISA card would be debited against the Bache account. In addition, the user of a Bache Command Account will be able to obtain year-end statements that would tally any checks written for tax-deductible items and have a sweep arrangement whereby idle cash in a Bache account would be automatically placed into a money market fund, a tax exempt securities fund, or a government securities fund, depending on the customer's choice.[10]

Prudential Capital and Investment Services, Inc., a Prudential Insurance Co. of America subsidiary, signed a definitive agreement to buy a $25 million asset, Capital City Bank of Hapeville, Georgia. The acquisition requires approval of the FDIC, banking and insurance regulators in Georgia, and insurance regulators in New Jersey, Prudential's home state. The Prudential bank will concentrate on deposit-gathering activities on longer-term certificates and the popular money market accounts. On its asset side, the bank may go into the business of making six-digit credit-secured personal loans, making equity loans, and offering consumer leasing services. The bank expected to sell its demand deposit and commerical loans to someone else so that the Prudential acquisition will not fall under the restriction of the Bank Holding Company Act. A Prudential executive has described the purchase as a defensive move in the sense that the company was fearful that Congress would prohibit such consolidations, but only after Prudential competitors had added depository institutions to their operations. In that case, Prudential would be "grandfathered out" of the deposit-taking business while others were "grandfathered in." It is not the original intention of Prudential to create a financial supermarket. However, if the Sears experiment to put financial centers into the companies retail stores proves successful, Prudential might seek to set up shopping mall locations.

CIGNA

While Prudential-Bache and Shearson/American Express mergers appear to focus on selling new financial and insurance products to individuals at retail, the Connecticut General–INA union (CIGNA) is aimed at corporate customers. It represents the long-range strategy of seeking to sell group insurance coverage to individuals through their employers. The combination of INA's products in health, automobile, and property coverage with Connecticut General's establishment position in corporate employee benefit plans offers much promise. Group coverage for auto, home, and health insurance sold to individuals through employee benefit programs will have lower premiums and lower operating costs. INA's international arm should help expand Connecticut General's presence in the multinational corporate arena. This acquisition involves more than the typical buying-for-value concept, as both of these companies were looking for ways to diversify their assets and marketing ability and to avoid an unfriendly takeover by a noninsurer.

Since the merger, CIGNA has purchased a 40 percent interest in a start-up Asian investment bank, a partial interest in a small trade finance company with a far eastern group, and a large British insurance company specializing in life insurance. This latter investment should complement INA's international insurance operations, giving the insurance giant a stronger foothold abroad. CIGNA Corp. announced an agreement in principal to acquire

American Foreign Insurance Association (AFIA), an international insurance underwriting association for $215 million in cash. By combining CIGNA's $1.1 billion in annual international insurance premiums with AFIA's $1 billion, CIGNA will move into a league with the American International Group, which is the world's largest international insurer, with $2.8 billion in international premiums. In AFIA, CIGNA gains a sixty-five-year-old organization with licenses to do business in sixty-three countries, has 4,700 employees and has broad expertise in numerous foreign markets. One of the most important parts of the acquisition for CIGNA was the net gain of twenty-three licenses that AFIA holds and CIGNA, which has fifty-seven licenses, does not. Together, the two will be able to sell insurance in eighty countries. Many of those additional licenses are in large growth markets such as Asia and Scandinavia, where CIGNA has been unsuccessful in gaining access because governments have stopped granting new licenses to foreign insurers. CIGNA has made a strategic determination that the international market for insurance products is probably better than the domestic market because of higher profit margins and superior growth prospects.

CIGNA has also entered a joint venture with United Motor Works, a Malaysian trading company, to create an international trade finance company, CIGNA UMW Finance. The Los Angeles-based venture will provide such services as export finance, letters of credit, trust receipt, and bankers acceptance financing. The company will concentrate on trade finance among the United States, the Far East and Europe, particularly assistance to U.S. companies entering the export market.

According to Wall Street analysts, CIGNA has considered over the past three years the purchase of a Swiss bank, a specialized leasing company, and greater involvement in wholesale corporate banking with a London connection. Venture capital-type communications companies, payroll processing companies, and an investment management company might also be found on the menu of potential future acquisitions. However, many of these expansion plans may be delayed because of poor underwriting results in its property/ casualty division.

CIGNA remains primarily a multiline insurance company with a major role in life insurance, employee benefit plans, and property casualty lines. Among U.S. companies it has one of the largest international operations. The merger, originally announced as a merger of equals, has turned out to be an acquisition by Connecticut General of INA Corp. Most members of the INA executive management team have resigned with their multiyear golden parachute contracts in force.

JCPenney Co.

JCPenney Co. is another retailer entering the war of the financial service centers through an agreement with First Nationwide Savings. As a result of recent acquisitions this savings and loan association has 150 branches in California, New York, and Florida. First Nationwide intends to set up financial service centers in five Penney stores in northern California on a test basis. If the program is successful, more centers would probably follow. Penney's actions follow in the footsteps of Sears. Soon it may be difficult to separate retailing from retail commercial services.

The Penney centers will be 1,500 square foot "environments" that will combine the sale of First Nationwide deposit accounts and loans with the activities of Penney's insurance companies. JCPenney already has 107 insurance sales centers in its 1,700 stores. Those centers sell life, health, automobile, and homeowners' insurance through the centers and directly to credit cardholders. Penney has 25 million cardholders, 16 million of whom are active users of the Penney card. First Nationwide's money market account and other financial products will be sold through the mail to Penney cardholders. First Nationwide may also sell tax preparation services at these financial service centers, individual retirement accounts, mortgages, and other loans.

In April 1983 JCPenney announced that it agreed to acquire the $28 million asset First National Bank of Harrington in Delaware. If approved by the regulatory authorities, it could provide a vehicle for the retailer to strengthen its move into consumer financial services. The acquisition may also fit into Penney's moves to "capitalize on existing in-house expertise." Just prior to the bank announcement, Penney had signed agreements with Shell Oil Co. and Gulf Oil Corp. under which Penney's nationwide electronic communications network will be used to transmit credit authorization and transaction data for the oil companies' service stations. JCPenney has also purchased a majority interest in First Hand, an experimental videotex program begun in the upper Midwest by First Bank Systems of Minneapolis. Videotex is a home banking and two-way communication medium. It offers the potential for retail sales to the consumer at home.

Aetna

Aetna Life & Casualty Company, the nation's largest stockholder-owned insurance company, has been moving rapidly into the financial services market and into some nonfinancial fields. The company acquired an 86 percent interest in Federated Investors, an investment company with $27 billion under management. Federated is mainly a manager of money market funds that it oversees for bank trust departments. It also provides banks with discount stock brokerage service and "sweep" facilities that allow banks to automatically invest checking account balances above a certain level in money market funds. In addition, Aetna has purchased a 40 percent interest in Samuel Montagu, a British merchant bank. The Federated and Montagu transactions show Aetna's desire to carve out a niche in providing financial services to corporations and financial institutions in the United States and abroad. The Aetna approach is different from the approach used by some rival insurance companies that have bought securities firms with big retail networks that serve individuals. Aetna has also made major acquisitions and investments in the energy and communications industries. Geosource and Satellite Business systems represented their major interests in oil servicing and communications satellites. However, Aetna elected to get rid of Geosource in 1984 because it had not been as profitable as expected. The company also has been a major participant in oil and gas exploration programs. In addition, Aetna is a major real estate investor and developer. Real estate has so far proved to be the most profitable of its major diversification moves to date.

Aetna Life & Casualty Company's Federated Investors subsidiary has applied to form a state-chartered, non-Federal Reserve System member bank to be called the Federated Bank & Trust Company in Parsippany–Troy Hills, New Jersey. To avoid qualifying as a bank, the Federated Bank plans to eschew commercial loans but accept demand deposits. It will have trust and fiduciary powers as well. Thus Aetna would join the growing number of insurers, such as Prudential and Travelers Corp., seeking a more direct role in banking.

It is important to note that insurance operations still account for over 80 percent of Aetna's sales despite its major diversification effort. Employee benefit plans accounted for close to 60 percent of the 1982 revenues and 83 percent of profits.

Transamerica

Although the McFadden Act of 1927 prohibits interstate branching, the law does not prohibit a bank holding company from owning banks in more than one state. As a matter of fact, the Transamerica Corporation was established in 1928 to circumvent the McFadden Act. Transamerica owned banks in eleven western states by 1956.

The Bank Holding Company Act of 1956 prohibits the interstate acquisition of banks by holding companies, except for acquisitions specifically permitted under the laws of the acquired bank's state. The act also restricted the activities in which bank holding companies could engage through their affiliates but contained a "grandfather" clause permitting existing bank holding companies to continue in business.

As a result of the 1956 Bank Holding Company Act, Transamerica was split into two companies. One of the companies owned only banks and was called Firstamerica when it began business in 1958. This name was changed twice—to Western Bancorporation in 1961 and to First Interstate Bancorp in 1981. As a matter of fact, each of its twenty-one banks is called First Interstate Bank (Los Angeles), First Interstate Bank (Portland), and so on.

The other part of the spin-off was and still is called Transamerica Corporation. This diversified financial services corporation owns Occidental Life and affiliated insurance companies, a motion picture company, a car rental company (Budget), and an airline charter company, among others.

Xerox Corp.

To broaden its role in the financial services industry, Xerox Corp. has acquired Van Kampen Merritt, a major wholesaler of tax-exempt unit investment trusts. Xerox offered $150 million, plus an earnings-based contingent payment of up to $68 million over three years, for the privately owned investment banker. Van Kampen, with $7 billion in trust assets outstanding, packages the trusts for regional brokers who sell them under their own labels. Xerox has chosen not to go into the retail securities business, preferring instead to wholesale innovative, packaged financial products. This is the second large purchase in the financial services industry for Xerox, which in early 1983 paid $1.6 billion for Crum and Forster, a large property casualty insurer. Less than a year after Xerox took it over, Crum and Forster agreed to acquire an insurance holding company named Navco for $34 million. Xerox has also made a 25 percent investment in the Bond Insurance Group, a company similar to Municipal Bond Insurance Association (MBIA) and Financial Guaranty Insurance Co. (FGIC), companies that insure municipal bonds and taxable instruments.

Xerox Credit Corporation, a major equipment lessor, lends funds to both Xerox customers as well as others seeking equipment financing. The Xerox Corporation is establishing a separate financial services division to include Crum and Forster, Van Kampen Merritt, and the Xerox Credit Corporation. David T. Kearns, Xerox's president, told securities analysts that his goal was to maintain one-third of Xerox's income from the financial services sector. In the future, the financial services group is expected to expand at the same rate as Xerox's traditional office equipment business. In the future, the financial services group would probably not grow through acquisition of new businesses but by developing those already in the company, according to Melvin Howard, president of the financial services division.

American Can Co.

American Can Co. engages in consumer products distribution, insurance, packaging, chemicals, and resource recovery. Operations include Fingerhut (direct marketing), the Musicland Group and Pickwick Distribution (sale of prerecorded music and related products), plastics packaging, retort pouches, metal cans, recovery of aluminum, and manufacturing of polyethelene. However, acquisitions in the financial service area have been so rapid that American Can's insurance companies combined are now among the top five writers of annual insurance volume in the United States.

The insurance business should expand further when American exercises its option to acquire two-thirds ownership and 80 percent voting interest in Ticor for close to $270 million from Southern Pacific Corporation. Ticor is one of the largest writers of mortgage insurance in the country. American Can also has an option to purchase the remaining one-third interest at a later date.

American Can purchased Associated Madison Companies, an insurance holding company best known for its mail order sales to credit cardholders and other affinity groups through its National Benefit Life label. A few months later the company purchased Transport Life Insurance Company which specializes in credit and universal life. Shortly thereafter, American Can purchased Penncorp Financial, a general insurance counseling firm. This purchase was followed by the acquisition of a 7.5 percent interest in Paine Webber, one of the few remaining independent, nationwide stockbrokers.

Chairman William Woodside has indicated that a substantial number of acquisitions are planned in the years ahead in the financial services area and that there will continue to be divestiture of low margin, modestly profitable noninsurance operations. The financial services group is under the control of Gerald Tsai of mutual fund fame.

ITT

Harold Geneen, the legendary conglomerate builder of the 1960s and 1970s, molded ITT into a $21 billion giant. Today, ITT is a conglomerate with 27 percent of its 1983 revenues coming from telecommunications, 24 percent from manufacturing, 12 percent from food and home products, 25 percent from insurance, and 12 percent from other services. As a percentage of 1983 profits, 29 percent came from insurance, 26 percent other services, 22 percent telecommunications, 15 percent manufacturing, and 8 percent food and products.

Its insurance and information operations include the Hartford Insurance Group and the electronic mail system used by the White House. ITT also owns Sheraton hotels, Scott lawn products, Rayonier forest products, and ITT Financial Services. ITT has a major presence in computers, telephones, switching equipment, windshield wipers, turbines, and valves. Despite a presence in the aforementioned businesses, ITT has sold off more than sixty-five companies (raising about $1.2 billion) under the reign of current chairman, Rand Araskog. Wall Street analysts would not be surprised if the company sold the Rayonier division, Sheraton, and some of the auto parts companies since some of these cyclical companies may be approaching an earnings peak in 1984 to 1985.

Can Financial Conglomerates Succeed?

With a loosening of regulation, financial conglomerates could emerge that offer a full range of financial services nationwide. It is also possible that nationwide banking will become permissible before too long and that the separation of investment and commercial banking powers will no longer be required by the Glass-Steagall Act. Regulations that presently separate insurance companies, banks, and consumer finance and investment brokerages are being eroded, laying the foundations for the future. The real questions that must be answered are whether U.S. consumers will really be attracted by one-stop shopping for all their financial needs and whether the environment is truly different today so that hybrid financial products and cross-selling across subsidiaries can really work in the 1980s. Recently, the advertising of financial services seems to encourage consumers to be selective, to pick and choose the best investment or vendor of services to fit a particular need.

Cross-selling synergies are expected to be evolutionary. The true test of synergism will come over the next few years when we shall see whether the diverse parts of these financial-service conglomerates can mesh with one another. If these synergies do not work, then the small independent bank or financial boutique will not be threatened. It is not clear that there really are economies of scale at the giant banks or financial conglomerates. Moreover networking and franchising might substitute for financial conglomerates.

There are also some cultural differences between investment bankers, commercial bankers, discount brokers, insurance executives, and retailers that involve compensation and reaction time. Are current organizations and culture compatible with realizing synergistic benefits? Proper compensation, retraining of the sales force, and a continual flow of new products may be necessary if cross-selling of financial services is to be successful. Can financial service providers see eye to eye on the sales floor—or in the brokerage office or branch office?

The jury is still out on whether or not financial conglomerates are on the whole going to be successful. If cross-selling of financial services works or if economies of scale can be found then of course these conglomerates have a better chance of surviving and prospering. On the other hand, history has shown that many such ventures have not worked in the past. Greyhound, Armco, and other large corporations have found a lack of synergy in their financial service acquisitions.

The home computer supplemented with a financial services modem or an attachment to a cable system has the potential to offer the consumer the ability to bank, invest, purchase insurance, and buy goods and services at home at discount prices using a debit or credit card—if it can be made financially feasible. This type of system can certainly replace the need for a financial supermarket located in a retail store or at a bank branch. Is the consumer interested in price or one-stop convenience for financial services?

The answers to at least some of these questions are negative for effective synergy, according to recent evidence. The best scenarios of the financial conglomerates may not be able to be played out successfully, and it is not at all certain that additional free-market accidents, such as the fiasco at Continental Illinois, during the next year or so will not impel lawmakers to reverse the trend toward liberalization of structural constraints.

Notes

1. A. Gart, *An Insider's Guide to the Financial Services Revolution* (New York: McGraw Hill, 1984), p. 37.

2. *Ibid.*, pp. 37–38.

3. *Ibid.*, p. 39.

4. *Ibid.*, p. 42.

5. *Business Week*, Nov. 16, 1981, pp. 142–143.

6. Gart, p. 46.

7. *Ibid.*, p. 47.

8. *Ibid.*, p. 49.

9. Walter Wriston, in "Banking in Transition," *Banker's Magazine*, Sept./Oct. 1978, p. 35.

10. Gart, pp. 50–51.

5
Some Problems and Solutions

Both the thrifts and the commercial and savings banks have received substantial media attention because they have experienced a record number of failures and forced mergers. We begin this chapter by examining the nature of the problems of the thrifts and of small, independent banks. We then look at some potential solutions to these problems and offer suggestions on how to improve earnings at these financial institutions. Techniques to be considered include the conversion of mutual thrifts to stockholder-owned companies, the use of adjustable-rate mortgages, swapping fixed-rate deposits for adjustable-rate deposits, the use of hedging techniques, the selling or buying of branches, and offering discounts on outstanding low-yielding mortgages to encourage their early retirement.

We then turn our attention to the problems and challenges of the insurance industry. The life insurers have seen their old bread and butter policy—the whole life policy—diminish in popularity as variable and universal life policies came into vogue. Profits have eroded as distribution and other expenses spiral upwards. The property and casualty insurers have also sustained increased operating expenses and record underwriting losses. We consider a number of suggestions for controlling operating expenses, look at some potential diversification opportunities, and then briefly consider the advantages and disadvantages of demutualization.

The Recent Restructuring of the Thrift Industry

Within the past five years, the economic viability of the traditional structure of savings and loans has been permanently destroyed by a combination of record-high interest rates and volatile unstable interest rate fluctuations. Competitive pressures, never before a factor in this industry, virtually have forced a total change in management methods, strategies, and approaches. The first step in accomplishing the restructuring process was recognizing its necessity. The search for new methods to ensure economic viability of the industry focused attention on two role models: mortgage banking and commercial banking. As it happened, the larger thrifts have generally moved in the direction of commercial banking; the smaller have concentrated strongly in mortgage banking. Both groups have made greater use of the secondary mortgage market. They now sell newly generated fixed-rate mortgages into the secondary market, concentrating on maximizing front-end origination fees, which have evolved into a significant source of revenue. Many of the larger thrifts have acquired mortgage servicing companies and are purchasing from other thrifts the servicing apsects of their mortgage portfolios. This new activity provides a stable source of continuing revenue, the profitability of which is impervious to interest rate fluctuations. As a further defense against interest rate volatility, the successful survivors are increasingly emphasizing the use of adjustable-rate mortgages (ARMs).

Historically, thrifts issued long-term fixed-rate mortgages that were funded by short-term borrowings. So long as regulation controlled the rates payable by thrifts and their competitors, savings depositors remained relatively stable. However, early in the decade, new market forces arose—nondepository competitors such as money market funds—and began to pay market interest rates to smaller savers. The thrifts remained constrained by the old rules. The process known as disintermediation set in quickly; the outflow from the thrifts was quick and ruthless. To stem the tide, the thrifts were permitted to increase rates payable to depositors. Now the thrifts found that their cost of funds had increased by several percentage points while their low-yield, fixed-rate, long-term mortgage portfolio dragged them into disaster that was an industrywide problem. The result of this interest rate exposure mismatch was that 1,000 savings and loan institutions failed in the period 1980 to 1983.

In response to these widely perceived problems, the Federal Home Loan Bank Board and the Congress adopted regulatory and legislative changes that provided better tools to manage interest rate risk. For the first time, thrifts were authorized

1. To lend on the security of adjustable-rate mortgages;
2. To engage in short-term consumer lending, formerly the prerogative of commerical banks and specialized, licensed lending institutions;
3. To engage in commercial lending, formerly the prerogative of commercial banks.

Theoretically, these new powers have the potential to revolutionize the industry. However, before the revolution takes hold, the existing portfolios must be retired. This can be done slowly or very slowly, but it cannot be done quickly. There are other techniques available to speed the process. For example, it is possible to sell off the old mortgages (replacing them with ARMs, consumer and commercial loans) but this requires the thrift to recognize a capital loss.

Since the capital position, even of the largest institutions, is often not too robust, this quick-fix solution is not possible because its effect will be to reduce the institution's net-worth–to–asset ratio below regulatory standards. Besides, some thrift managers still want to continue to make some long-term fixed-rate mortgages because, with a deeply sloped yield curve, if the mortgages are funded by short-term deposits, there are good profits to be earned, at least in the short-run and so long as rates necessary to maintain the deposits do not fly through the roof. It is just that possibility, however, that makes funding long-term fixed-rate assets with variable-rate short-term deposits an extremely risky business.[1]

There is no one correct way to restructure. The major decision faced by thrifts is whether to restructure, to the extent possible, existing portfolios in one stroke, or to do so incrementally as assets and liabilities mature. Generally, it is counterproductive to reduce interest rate risk by locking in negative spreads or to eliminate net worth by selling assets at large losses. The trick is to allow only those gaps where the returns are sufficient to compensate for the risk exposure. There are several choices:[2]

1. As stated above, it is sometimes possible to restructure the portfolio by selling at discount long-term fixed-rate mortgages and replacing them with assets that reprice more frequently, such as ARMs and consumer loans.

2. On the liability side, it is frequently possible to roll existing short-term liabilities into longer-term liabilities. Where this is possible, the effect can be dramatic. When the yield curve is positively sloped, any reduction of asset/liability maturity mismatches involves difficult trade-offs between risks and returns. But it is usually more costly to issue longer-term deposits than to have shorter-term deposits. There is also the additional risk that if rates increase to considerably higher levels, consumers will accept a modest interest rate penalty and cash in their longer-term certificates prior to the original maturity.

3. One way to avoid interest-rate risk is to match the repricing date of the asset with that of the liability. Another way is to hedge the institution's balance sheet so that it is immune to vicissitudes of swings in interest rates. Practically speaking, it is impossible to exorcise all risk from the business and still make a profit. But it is possible to reduce interest-rate risk to an acceptable level. As a rule, management should avoid attempting to eliminate all interest-rate risk, because in a declining interest-rate environment, the institution would lose the potential profit opportunities to be made on the sale of long-term fixed-rate assets (particularly mortgages and bonds) that would inevitably occur, because prices for these instruments are inversely related to interest-rate movements.

The important task is to shrink the maturity imbalance between the two sides of the balance sheet. Restructuring, however, is expensive and generally involves the potential sacrifice of near-term profits. In this negative environment, it is difficult for a thrift institution to give up the potential for current earnings. The absence of substantial net worth does not really allow these thrifts to pass up near-term earnings or to take actual losses. To complicate the restructuring process, customers may not be buying what the institution needs to sell.

The ARM has been the principal new product that has enabled thrifts partially to restructure the asset side of the balance sheet. It may take an additional period of five years, but interest-rate risk will be reduced substantially by 1990 as ARMs go on the books, as thrifts gradually sell off fixed-rate assets when the interest-rate window allows, and as maturing assets are paid down.

Adjustable-Rate Mortgages

Until a few years ago, home buyers did not worry about making choices between various types of mortgages. The fixed-rate twenty-to-thirty-year maturity was the only type available. Today, there are a number of options. The adjustable-rate mortgage (ARM) has become extremely popular. Only a few years after its introduction, it accounts nationally for about two-thirds of new residential mortgages. ARMs are popular with borrowers because, in the first year, the interest rate and therefore the monthly payment is lower. This first-year discount ranges from 1.0 to 2.5 percentage points, which on a typical $50,000 mortgage translates into initial monthly savings of $50 to $125 per month. The drawbacks of ARMs to borrowers is that the interest rate will fluctuate over the life of the mortgage, which means that at some point, usually the most inopportune moment, it will go up. Typically, an adjustment of rates will be made annually, biannually, or triannually with a cap of two points increase per adjustment period and a five-point maximum aggregate over the life of the mortgage. Notwithstanding the danger inherent in the ARM, for a young person who anticipates a career move within a few years, or who expects regular increases in income, variable-rate mortgage with a low initial "teaser" rate may be the best borrowing strategy.

Historically, conventional fixed-rate mortgages have been the lifeblood of savings and loans. But the practice of carrying large portfolios of fixed-rate mortgages was the major factor contributing to several years of losses and the erosion of net worth across the entire thrift industry. Under conditions of rising and volatile interest rates, in a climate of deregulation, a unique conveyance of conditions, the income generated from the typical fixed-rate mortgage portfolio was not sufficient to cover the rising cost of funds and associated expenses. When the passbook account was the major source of funds, fixed-rate lending made good sense because the rate spread between the passbook rate and the fixed-rate mortgage was not only attractive but was assured by regulation. When a variety of investment instruments paying market rates became available to consumers, they shifted their deposits out of passbook accounts and into these higher-yielding investments such as certificates of deposit (CDs), time deposits, and money market funds. To compete—that is, to attract deposits at maturity—the thrifts had to raise their own rates to depositors. This reintermediation of funds, drastically narrowed or wiped out the spread between the cost of funds and the income from the old mortgage portfolio.

The problem with carrying fixed-rate mortgages in portfolio is that there exists an interest rate risk: that is, if interest rates rise, the value of the fixed-rate mortgages already closed declines. While the income generated from these mortgages remains constant, the cost of funds to the lender will assuredly increase when interest rates rise. This does not mean that fixed-rate mortgage lending should be eliminated entirely. At times, interest rates may be expected to fall, in which case the spread will increase and the portfolio will become more valuable. Under such conditions, it is possible to generate capital gains by the simple expedient of selling all or part of the mortgage portfolio. Therefore, some high-yielding fixed-rate mortgages should be kept in portfolios as a diversification move.

As a general rule, however, fixed-rate mortgage loans should be priced at the Federal National Mortgage Association (FNMA) or Federal Home Loan Mortgage Corporation (Freddie Mac) rate, plus adjustments for servicing. They can then be sold at par in the secondary market without a loss, while the originating lender earns the origination and settlement points.

Depending on location, between 60 and 80 percent of new residential mortgages are adjustable-rate mortgages. The ARM eliminates some of the interest-rate risk associated with fixed-rate mortgages because the rate periodically adjusts to an index that is generally tied to a treasury note index or a cost of funds index such as the one compiled by the Federal Home Loan Bank Board.

The ARM is not without its problems. It is important to maintain underwriting standards that concentrate on the monthly payments to be made after the first adjustment when the real, rather than the initial, teaser rate first takes effect. But even underwriting is subject to competitive pressures. An initial teaser rate that is too low can be unprofitable, while an initial rate that is too high will be resisted. Origination and settlement points earned on an ARM are generally similar to those earned on a conventional fixed-rate mortgage, and frequently receipt of this income provides a substantial kick in the right direction to the lenders profit and loss statement. In the repricing year of an ARM, the rate on the loan might be set at 1.75 or two percentage points above the rate for a one-year or three-year treasury note. Usually, by contract, the rate change will not exceed two percentage points in any one year or five percentage points in the aggregate during the lifetime of the loan. This means that even if treasury rates rise by as much as six or seven percentage points in one year, the mortgage rate increase is restrained by the contractual cap. Conversely, the interest rate paid to the lender will decline if the yield on treasury notes declines. However, if rates are declining, one can expect the lender's basic cost of funds to be declining so that a variable-rate mortgage is not counterproductive to its profit potential. The ARM protects the mortgage lender against rising interest rates and helps to prevent the erosion of capital and surplus over the long run if interest rates rise. If the strategy that suggests selling most fixed-rate mortgages is utilized, there is little risk of another interest-rate trap. Maturities of assets and liabilities come into closer balance, and the institution should be capable of holding a more liquid position to meet mortgage demand without straining any of the regulatory ratios. However, managers should be aware that it may take as much as five years or even more before the total income received from a variable-rate mortgage will match the income received from a fixed-rate mortgage because of the difference in first-year interest rates.

The House Banking Committee has held hearings on alleged abuse of the ARM concept, focusing on teaser rates, payment shock, and negative amortization. Therefore, it is important that the lending industry set underwriting standards that are not based on a teaser rate and that borrowers are informed of the full extent of possible monthly payment increases under a worse-case interest-rate scenario. Lenders that offer initial promotional interest rates on their ARMs must ensure that borrowers do not unknowingly face the danger of "payment schock" and that all loans are properly underwritten. The lender must not delude itself about the amount of interest-rate risk protection that is attached to an ARM. There is nothing wrong with reasonable initial rate discounts or negative amortization. However, the lender must protect itself from any lowering of underwriting standards and still make certain that the rate offered in the first year is profitable.

Thrifts and Consumer Lending

Banks have been involved in consumer lending for more than a century, but it is a relatively new field for most thrift institutions. A consumer loan portfolio is of much shorter-term duration than a typical residential mortgage portfolio. It offers the same diversification, the same opportunity to intermix fixed- and variable-rate contracts, and greater opportunity to attract and hold customers. It is a business worth being in, but certain classes of consumer loans pose greater dangers than others. The neophyte consumer lender should beware of lending on the security of mobile homes or used U.S-made automobiles that are more than three or four years old.

The safest and perhaps the best way to get started in the consumer loan business is to draw from the institution's own base of home mortgage borrowers and depositors. These two classes generally will provide the lowest default ratios. This group can be targeted for credit card loans, new automobile loans, and checks drawn against a preset maximum line of credit collateralized by the equity in the already existing home mortgage. In entering the consumer loan business, it is most important that appropriate underwriting standards be established and followed. It is equally important that modern, efficient operational methods be initiated and maintained. No mortgage-oriented institution should attempt to enter the consumer loan business without adding to its staff an appropriate number of people experienced in that type of lending. A beginner might also expect to sustain some degree of operating loss during the phase-in period, so a sufficiency of capital should be assured before the attempt is made. However, high-quality consumer loans will provide a diversified short-term portfolio of assets that will help to counter balance the necessity of depending on the continuing stability of the home mortgage market.

Asset/Liability Management

When managers were able, with historical justification, to anticipate narrow interest-rate movements over extremely long time periods, a lender had to be concerned only with matching the amount of funds available for lending with loan demand. Interest rates were set to provide a spread sufficient to cover operating costs and profits. The success of the operation was a mathematical certainty as long as the loan was repaid.

In the current economy, the profitable matching of funds available for lending with funds placed on loan (a process referred to as asset/liability management or ALM) is not simple. If a mistake is made today, the result can be catastrophic. The concept of being exposed to risk of operating loss is something new to thrift lenders. Potential profits depend on accurate projections of interest rate fluctuations and the use of financial strategies not even dreamed of under the old methods. The modern thrift manager must be attuned to those new concepts of business, but a well-run ALM program will provide an accurately quantified profit/risk assessment, which will aid immensely in arriving at correct (profitable) management decisions.

The basic problem to be rectified by an ALM program is the traditional borrow-short/lend-long structure of savings and loan institutions—that is, the mismatch of short-term deposits and long-term loans. The critical point is that thrifts are always betting that interest rates will decline whenever they borrow at short-term variable rates and lend at long-term fixed rates. The solution to the problem lies in a combination of activities. Cost of funds can be made more certain by solicitation of long-term time deposits, reducing dependency on shorter-term funds. Income can be made to follow cost of funds by utilization of adjustable-rate mortgages and shorter-term commercial and consumer loans. To the extent that these techniques do not do the job, the institution may adjust any remaining discrepancies by hedging in interest rate futures and options markets and by engaging in interest rate swaps. These latter techniques should not be considered primary sources of income. They should be utilized only to adjust temporary interest rate imbalances in existing portfolios and should be terminated when the imbalances are corrected. A word of caution is appropriate. These techniques are inherently highly leveraged specialized financial transactions and, when used improperly, offer great potential for immense loss. No institution should attempt to use these techniques unless the program is supervised by a highly experienced and responsible executive.

In principal, it is best to relate the economic terms of loans (assets) and funds available (liabilities) to market conditions especially if there is to be a maturity mismatch. In other words, buy the cheaper assets (that is, issue loans at the highest rates possible) even when their maturities do not coincide with the maturities of the liabilities. But flexibility must always be the watchword. If, at any given time, the liability side offers opportunity, raise as much money as possible at the extremely favorable rates then available, and take care of the mismatch problems by resorting to the adjustment techniques. The idea is to immunize net worth from changing market conditions by causing the market values of assets and liabilities to move together as interest rates change. Under extremely restrictive conditions, maintaining the same duration on both sides will achieve the desired result. Otherwise, the use of adjustment techniques is a necessity.

Swaps

Steven J. Goldstein, deputy director of the Office of Policy and Economic Research of the Federal Home Loan Bank, has stated that portfolio hedging can better be accomplished with cash market instruments and interest rate swaps rather than by hedging with futures. Goldstein suggests that a thrift has three methods available to lock-in long-term cost of funds:

1. Long-term deposits;
2. Long-term advances; and
3. Long-term interest rate swaps.

In the first two techniques, while the cost is locked-in, the matched income is not, and a positive spread is never guaranteed. Interest rate swaps provide this extra advantage, and proper use virtually guarantees a profit.

In an interest rate swap, the savings association agrees to make a long-term fixed-rate interest payment to a swap partner, receiving in return a variable-rate payment tied to a short-term market interest rate. If the swap is used to hedge a long-term fixed-rate mortgage portfolio, the thrift passes the interest payments from the mortgage portfolio through to the swap partner and uses the variable-rate payments received from the swap partner to pay the interest due to short-term depositors. Asset/liability managers are now in a better position to regularly evaluate and adjust their interest rate sensitivities. The interest received from the swap partner fluctuates with the thrift's cost of short-term deposits, while the interest payment made by the thrift to the swap partner is fixed at a level equal to no more than the yield received from the mortgage portfolio.[3] Thus, the interest rate swap enables the thrift to provide consumers with long-term fixed-rate mortgages without itself taking much of an interest rate risk.

Let us consider a swap between a multinational foreign bank and a savings and loan. Suppose that the bank is able to lend at 100 basis points over LIBOR and to raise funds at LIBOR (London Interbank Offer Rate) plus 12.5 basis points. Suppose that the bank also wishes to take advantage of an interest rate window and to raise five-year funds in the Eurobond market at a rate of 13 percent. The bank then converts that fixed-rate borrowing into a floating-rate obligation by agreeing to swap interest rates, by making payments to the thrift at LIBOR minus 12.5 basis points. Because the LIBOR rate is usually considerably higher than the thrift's MMDA rate, the savings and loan is pleased to receive a rate of LIBOR minus 12.5 basis points that will enable it to pay its MMDA interest rate expenses. On the other hand, the savings and loan agrees to make a fixed-rate payment sufficient to cover the cost of servicing the multinational 13 percent Eurobond debt.

The thrift, which possesses many mortgages that yield 13 percent or more, ends up paying what is owed to the multinational's bondholders and receiving a floating-rate yield greater than the cost of servicing its own liabilities. The U.S. thrift makes an arbitrage gain, while erasing the maturity gap between its long-term loan and its shorter liabilities. The multinational bank has lowered its funding cost from LIBOR plus one-eighth to LIBOR minus one-eighth.

In swap transactions, no exchange of principal takes place, and no securities change hands between the two parties; each party remains legally liable for all the payments of its external financing. With no transfer of principal in an interest rate swap, credit risk is limited to the payment being exchanged over the term of the contract—that is, the servicing of the debt. If credit protection is desired, this can be accomplished through the use of an intermediary that guarantees the payment streams through a backup letter of credit, through the provision of collateral, and so forth.

There are definite advantages in using interest rate swaps, such as:

Speed of execution;

No disclosure or registration;

Single documentation;

Easy unwinding procedures;

Silent financing;

Increased liquidity and collateral;

The growth of an active secondary market for swaps;

Flexibility of size and maturity.

There are potential disadvantages, which include:

Roll-over risk;

Basis and market risk;

Credit risk.

Converting a mortgage loan portfolio to a securities portfolio is not the same as changing a $20 bill for two $10 bills because the swap incurs costs, has long-term operational impacts, requires sophisticated analytic techniques germane to economic feasibility, and requires exercise of various business disciplines. An interest rate swap enables each participant to alter the structure of its existing debt or to create new financing on attractive terms. Both swapping parties can obtain cheaper fixed- and floating-rate financing because of credit quality differentiation and market accessibility for various credits between the fixed- and floating-rate markets, the money and capital markets, and the domestic and international markets. Typically, corporations can access the floating-rate market more cheaply than the fixed-rate market, while financial institutions have comparatively easier access to lower cost fixed-rate funds. However, corporations generally prefer fixed-rate financing, while banks and thrifts generally prefer floating- or variable-rate financing. By utilizing their individual strengths, both participants can obtain the amount of funding required while swapping liabilities.

Hedging and Futures

Even though there is an active secondary market for fixed-rate residential mortgages, and even though most thrifts have sustained losses in mortgage portfolios values because of interest rate erosion, thrifts cannot afford to realize the losses by selling their low-yielding, "underwater" mortgage portfolios at prevailing market yields because to do so would require recognition of those losses, which in turn would severely impact on book net worth. Nothing can be done with current portfolios except take the loss or hold on until the portfolio liquidates.

However, if the resale value of the portfolio had been hedged, then the financial blood bath that did occur could have been avoided. Essentially, protection is obtained by selling short the appropriate number of futures contracts that corresponds most closely with the mortgage assets. A decline in portfolio value caused by increased interest rates should be offset by profits on the futures contracts. However, the correlation between interest rate movements in the two variables is not perfect. The potential for loss cannot be eliminated entirely, but the potential for anything but an acceptable loss certainly can be eliminated.

Sophisticated financial institutions, such as banks and insurance companies use hedging techniques for the following purposes:

1. To improve liquidity;
2. To lock in yields on anticipated investments;
3. To generate a more consistent investment performance;
4. As part of the asset/liability management program.

Consider the following examples:[4]

1. When treasury bill futures offer higher yields than cash rates, the purchase of strips of successive delivery dates will secure a yield greater than that currently available in the cash market.
2. When a bank has determined the timing and amount of projected CD sales, it can sell an appropriate number of futures contracts and buy them in as the CDs are sold. The bank is able to fix its effective borrowing rate to the extent that CD and treasury bill rates correlate with each other.
3. Thrifts often use Ginnie Mae futures when they make advance commitments to buy or sell whole mortgage or mortgage-backed securities at a firm price. Without hedge protection, there is total exposure to the risk of loss during the time required to conclude the other side of the transaction.
4. If a manager knows that a given amount of funds will be available for reinvestment at a certain time in the future, and believes that interest rates will fall prior to the time that the investment funds will be available, he or she can lock-in current interest rates for the investment he intends to make in the future. The manager would buy the appropriate number of futures contracts, the profits on which should approximately offset the

higher cost of assets purchased at the future date. If, contrary to expectations, interest rates should rise, the extra profit generated by the higher rate obtained on the future investment will approximately offset the loss of the futures transaction. Thus, the investment result is impervious to interest rate fluctuations; the current yield is protected.

Thrift Conversions

Although the blood-bath period is now history, the thrifts have not restructured their balance sheets or rebuilt their strengths as rapidly as regulators had hoped. When stripped of goodwill, deferred losses, and capital income certificates, net worth is down sharply from prior levels and remains at undesirable and unacceptably low levels. At year end 1984, there were still a substantial number of large thrift institutions with negative net worth.

However, what really counts is not the balance sheet, but whether consumers maintain their confidence and keep deposits intact. Fortunately, thus far, depositors' confidence has not been substantially eroded.

In reaction to the dangerously low level of net worth, the FSLIC has proposed a new definition of insolvency. To replace the current regulation that declares a thrift insolvent when its net worth falls to zero, the FSLIC would like to concentrate more on an association's ability to generate cash and to pay its bills. Regardless of the accounting prop engaged in by the regulators, the ultimate success of their delaying action is dependent on how quickly and by how much the thrift industry improves its profits and restores its capital.[5]

If the regulators are able to buy enough time, in the regular course of business, the low-yielding mortgages will self-liquidate through maturity and early payoff. As thrifts learn to take profitable advantage of their newly minted broader powers to make consumer and commercial loans to become real estate developers, and to control interest rate mismatches through use of adjustable-rate mortgages and other techniques, profits should once again begin to flow on a regular basis. Additional help to this process could come from declining long-term mortgage rates and lower short-term rates, if such should eventuate.[6]

Both the regulators and the industry are impatient for the restructuring process to be completed. But everyone recognized that the process will take place only over a long period of years. In certain instances, the process can be accelerated through mergers and by conversion of mutuals to stock ownership.

New rules and regulations, adopted because of the recent turmoil in the financial services industry in general to help the special problems of the thrift industry in particular, have presented significant new opportunities in this regard. These new rules have facilitated the adoption of corporate structures better suited to profit-making entities and have created broader new powers to aid in profit-making outside of traditional consumer real estate financing activities. Congress and the regulators have also made easier the conversions of a mutual institution into a stockholder-owned corporation. Such a revision brings new opportunities for injection of capital, alliances with nonthrift businesses, broadening of the services offered, and incentive programs for management.[7]

Conversion offers the advantages of being able to raise true equity capital; lays the foundation for diversification of activities and affiliation with existing or new nonfinancial business enterprises through a holding company parent; and presents new devices and opportunities to motivate and compensate management. The most prominent disadvantages are the costs in both dollars and time of the conversion process itself and the need to comply with the ongoing reporting requirements of a publicly held company. Also, management could ultimately lose control of an institution as its stock is sold and passes to new control groups.[8]

Notwithstanding the disadvantages during 1983, some of the largest federally chartered savings and loans and savings banks switched from the mutual form of organization to the stock form. To provide necessary controls over this activity, the FHLBB has set up guidelines to prevent the windfall distribution of stock to account holders of converting mutuals because these stock distributions could serve as an incentive for investors to shift their funds from one mutual to another, threatening the financial stability of mutuals suffering from deposit withdrawals. The FHLBB guidelines include the following:

The market value of the shares is to be determined by an independent appraisal.

To be eligible, one must be an account holder at least ninety days before the plan is approved by the trustees.

A deposit holder's pro rata share should be a function of the relative amount of deposits held by an individual compared to the total deposits.

If all the shares offered in the subscription are not purchased, the shares may be offered to the public or to eligible depositors.

One school of thought suggests that the reserves and surplus accounts belong to the depositors and should be distributed to them. Other scholars argue that since depositors have no risk capital invested because accounts are insured, the reserves and surplus belong to either the insuring agency or to a charity. Their reasoning is that no one really has a clear moral or legal right to the reserve at the time of conversion. As a practical matter, however, if their assets are marked to market, most converting thrifts have little or no net worth, so the arguments become an irrelevancy. Except under supervisory transactions, and new sale-of-control conversions, all FSLIC conversions require that savers in a mutual be given their preemptive rights on a nonassignable basis, the first opportunity to buy securities.

Allan D. Housley, a Washington lawyer, has stated that "You can grow out of your problems by merger, but it must be planned growth, not unrestricted growth." On the same subject, Jonathan Gray of Sanford C. Bernstein & Co. has commented that the regulatory accounting practices used when thrift institutions merge have the effect of permitting the losses of one merger partner to end up as profits for the surviving institution.[9]

Regulators seem to favor the merger approaches to resolving the earnings problems of individual savings and loans because it conserves more of the assets of the insurance fund over the short run than alternative measures. Consolidation can cut fixed costs by reducing duplication of personnel and boards of directors and by eliminating redundant and unprofitable branches.

Accounting Methods

Because of the thrift industry's present low net-worth position, and its need for new capital, merger conversions will occur during the remainder of the decade. Therefore, it will be useful to review some of the accounting concepts related to that type of transaction. There are alternative accounting methods available. Some institutions will want the merger conversion accounted for under the "pooling of interests" method. Here, the key advantage is that the surviving institution obtains not only the additional capital generated by the stock offering, but also obtains and incorporates the book net worth of the disappearing institution. This method should be adopted when the acquired entity has net worth of some substance.

On the other hand, when there is limited net worth available at the institution to be merged, it might be preferable to adopt the purchase method of accounting. Under this accounting treatment, the net worth of the disappearing institution is eliminated, and its assets and liabilities are adjusted to current market values. If asset values exceed liabilities, and they often do, the balancing factor is a "goodwill" item placed on the asset side of the balance sheet. When the merger is consummated, assets such as long-term fixed-rate mortgages, which have already been marked-to-market, can now be sold at current market value without further erosion of net worth. However, for income tax purposes, a loss is reported, with concomitant tax advantage. This method of accounting is often preferred by entities desiring to restate asset values on their balance sheet. It really buys time for a thrift to place new assets on the books that will be more interest rate sensitive, and it permits the painless liquidation of low-yielding fixed-rate mortgage portfolios.

Insured savings and loans have a choice of accounting principles to utilize in the preparation of their financial statements. They may choose between generally accepted accounting principles (GAAP) and regulatory accounting practices (RAP).

The FHLBB has embraced a number of accounting policies that are departures from GAAP. Generally speaking, RAP policies are more liberal in the recognition of income than those for GAAP. As a result of the difficult operating climate faced by many FSLIC insured thrifts, many of these institutions have adopted RAP accounting. The major differences between RAP and GAAP are:[10]

1. *Loan origination fees*
   RAP — Acquisition credits in excess of 2 percent plus $400 (2½ percent plus $400 for construction loans) are to be deferred and amortized over a period not less than ten years.
   GAAP — Loan fees may be recognized to income to the extent that they offset the loan origination costs, with the remainder amortized to income using the interest method of amortization.

2. *Loss deferral on sale of loans and certain securities*
   RAP — Subject to definitional tests, associations may elect to defer losses on the sale of loans over the estimated remaining contractual maturity of the loans sold.
   GAAP — No literature permits the deferral and subsequent amortization of losses.

3. *Loan commitment fees*
   RAP — Fees received can be recognized as income as follows:

Commitment Period	*Maximum Income*
6 to 12 months	1%
12 to 18 months	1½%
Over 18 months	2%

   Any excess fees received are to be deferred and considered as additional and acquisition credits.
   GAAP — Commitment fee income should be recognized up to the amount of related commitment expenses. The balance of any fees received is to be deferred and recognized as follows:
   1. The interest rate of the loan is to be at the current market rate at the time the loan is originated—deferred fees are to be amortized over the commitment period using the straight-line method (floating-rate commitment).
   2. The interest rate of the loan is fixed at the time of the commitment—deferred fees to be amortized over the combined commitment period and the loan period. The straight-line

method should be used prior to the loan origination; the interest method should be used thereafter (fixed-rate commitment).

Also, a determination is to be made at the time the loan is originated. If the committed interest rate is less than the market rate, deferral and amortization as indicated above should be followed. If the committed rate of interest is equal to, or greater than, the market rate of interest (at the time of origination), then any unamortized deferred fee may be recognized as current income.

4. *Regulatory forbearance in certain regulatory mergers*

In a number of mergers the FHLBB has agreed to permit acquirors to report certain aspects of the merger on a basis other than GAAP. Where this has been done, there could be a material difference between RAP and GAAP:

Goodwill — Frequently the FHLBB permits amortization over a longer period than is permissible under GAAP.

Capital assistance — The FHLBB may permit an institution to credit cash assistance to net worth while GAAP requires that it be recorded as a reduction in goodwill.

Branch Purchases and Sales

The escalating volume of branch transactions in late 1981 and in 1982 coincided with a deterioration in the financial condition of many thrifts and the willingness of the Federal Home Loan Bank Board to permit savings and loans to book goodwill and to amortize goodwill as permitted under then-existing generally accepted accounting principles (GAAP). The need to deal with short-term earnings and net-worth problems was a key factor behind resale of many branches. Branch sellers were able to increase their net worth by selling branches where the deposits were valued at a premium. The transfer of these branches was structured to provide advantages to both the buyer and seller. Purchasers received assets that were usually valued at less than the branch deposits received. The excess of the value of the deposits over the value of the assets is designated as goodwill. Until the FASB accounting change of September 1982, such goodwill often was amortized for periods of up to forty years on a straight-line basis. The buyer's goodwill became a gain on the transaction from the seller's point of view. After September 1982 the amortization period was reduced substantially under both GAAP and regulatory accounting principles (RAP) to the maturity of the interest-bearing assets transferred along with the deposits to the seller.[11]

The sale of branches has proved to be popular for a number of thrift institutions. In addition to the typical marketing reasons for expansion or purchase of branches, there are some accounting and financial purposes that merit discussion. Let us consider a hypothetical branch with $10 million in savings accounts with an average cost of funds of 10 percent and with $9 million of fixed-rate mortgages (par value) with an 11 percent gross yield and a current market value of 70 cents on the dollar or $6.3 million. Let us assume that thrift A will purchase this branch from thrift B with no cash changing hands. If the branch building is owned, it is included as part of the deal, while if the branch is leased, the lease and all equipment are taken over by thrift A. However, thrift B will continue to service the loans at an annual fee of 37.5 basis points, so that the net yield on the mortgage portfolio to thrift A after servicing will be 10 5/8 percent.

Thrift A will receive income of $956,000 per year from the mortgage portfolio, but will incur $1 million of interest expense on deposits, plus operating expenses. When the mortgages are put onto the books of thrift A, $2.7 million ($9.0 − $6.3) can be amortized into income over twelve years, while goodwill can be amortized over approximately thirty years. This gives additional income of $225,000 per year and additional expenses of $90,000 per year, or a bookkeeping profit of $135,000, which more than makes up for the $44,000 negative interest spread and operational expenses. This treatment is highly favorable during the twelve-year period in which the portfolio discount is amortized into income, but there would be a theoretical negative income feature from years 13 through 30. This is not troublesome to a sophisticated manager. The loss can then be made up because time is provided to enlarge the branch. A good branch should be able to double its asset size within any given five-year period.

There are also some benefits to thrift B, the seller of the branch. Thrift B is selling $9 million of assets at par that are really worth only $6.3 if marked to market. There are $10 million of deposits and $9 million of mortgage loans. Thrift B can immediately recognize as profit in the year of sale the $1 million difference. There is an additional $44,000 per year of transaction income saved by not having to make up from operations an existing negative interest spread. In addition, there is the income of (37.5 basis points), which will come to thrift B each year for servicing the mortgage portfolio.

There are, of course, other reasons for purchasing or selling branches. Branch purchases can be used as a means of entering new markets or strengthening positions in markets in which a thrift desired greater representation. It allows a thrift to better target the markets in which they want to be bigger or smaller competitors. Selective branch purchases can be used as a supplement to mergers and de novo branching in carrying out an effective geographic strategy. Branch sales can be used to exist from transactions where they are not earning a profit, cannot develop an adequate presence to become effective competitors, or lack the resources or desire to become an effective force.[12]

The large number of voluntary and involuntary mergers during the early 1980s resulted in the surviving institutions acquiring competing offices or offices in areas that the restructured institution does not wish to serve. The next few years will see a "rationalization" of branch coverage through the swapping of branches with other institutions, the buying or selling of branches, and the closing or merging of branches.

Sale of Mortgages

Let us consider the proposed sale of $10 million in conventional mortgage loans first under regular cost accounting and then under marked-to-market conditions. In the final case, let us consider the additional impact on the thrift of offering consumers a 10 percent discount on the repayment of their outstanding mortgages.

Assumptions

A. The average interest rate of $10 million in conventional mortgage loans is 9 percent, with twenty years until maturity, and an estimated market value of 73 percent of par.

$10 million at 9.00% =	$ 900,000	annual interest income
amortized loss over twenty-year average life ($2.7 million)	− 135,000	annual amortization
	$10,000,000	
	− 2,700,000	
Net proceeds from sale	$ 7,300,000	

B. It is assumed that the association will be able to reinvest in mortgages at an average rate of 13.50 percent.

$7.3 million × 13.50%	$ 985,500	
3% placement fee (only 2% plus $400 in immediate income unless sold; remainder to income over life)	219,000	
Total income on new funds	$ 1,204,500	
Less 9% on $10 million	− 900,000	
Amortization of loss	− 135,000	
Profit first year	$ 169,500	

The above computation is based on cost accounting. The loss of $2,700,000 will not be realized if the portfolio is marked-to-market and will allow an amortization of loss over thirty years in amortization of goodwill. A further profit or loss may be achieved if the sales price is plus or minus from the marked-to-market price at the time of conversion.

C. Now consider the case where a 10 percent discount is offered to existing mortgagors for early repayment of outstanding mortgages. If 5 percent of the customers accept the discount offer, then the institution would make an additional first-year profit consisting of the difference between being paid $.90 on the dollar and the market value of $.73 on the dollar. This $.17 per dollar for $500,000 of mortgages on a marked-to-market portfolio gives an additional first-year profit of $85,000. It should be noted that it is important to alert mortgagors who accept the discount offer that they will have to pay income tax on the discount given by the financial institution.

Other Opportunities for Thrifts

The savings and loan industry has considerable experience in real estate development and a cash flow staying power over the cycle that private real estate developers for the most part do not have. Thrifts have a great deal of experience in the actual building of homes for sale and can act as joint venture partners with builders, often improving on the builder's financial management. In some cases, they can accomplish the entire development alone. Some thrifts have even syndicated larger properties by sale of limited partnership interests, the thrift taking a typical front-end syndication profit. And, after a period of overbuilding in the 1983 to 1984 period, the commercial real estate market may provide new profit opportunities for some savings institutions.

Savings institutions and small banks must train employees to cross-sell more service to consumers and must raise current levels of compensation to attract personnel capable of success in this type of endeavor. There is no reason why the thrift industry should not consider offering services such as insurance, stock brokerage, and financial planning to consumers. There is no question that the level of competition that will be met will be new to the industry. However, the industries' access to its potential customer base gives it an advantage which should not be ignored.

In their build-up, IRA and Keogh accounts do not usually pay out interest earned, making their effective maturity equal to their stated maturity. People tend to add regularly to their retirement account at the same institution. This makes them among the most desirable and stable sources of longer-term funds, and the marketing of these programs should be an integral part of every institution's program.

Some banks and thrifts are offering to their IRA customers completion insurance programs, common-carrier and accidental death protection, discount telephone shopping services, discounts on hotel rooms, emergency cash services, and free financial newsletters. These offerings indicate that banks recognize how highly desirable these accounts are and emphasize retention as well as marketing programs. A number of financial institutions would rather compete in the marketplace by offering free insurance or some other give-away, rather than match the highest rate advertised in the local market. This type of offering for IRA account customers gives the bank a potential niche as well as an identification in the local marketplace.

Bank Performance

According to George H. Hempel, professor of finance at Southern Methodist University, the primary causes of the relatively poor performance of many banks are large credit losses, increased cost of funds, inadequate liquidity, and mismatched interest rate sensitivity. Except for the rising cost of funds, which is an external banking environment factor, these causes of poor performance were primarily and directly related to weak management practices. At some banks, management has been guilty of allowing rapid loan growth without adequate trained personnel and without ensuring proper loan documentation; overconcentration of the loan portfolio in one or two industries; limited or no verification of collateral; self-serving loans; paying no attention to country risk in the case of foreign loans; rewarding loan officers on the basis of the amount of loans booked without regard to quality; and not paying attention to how interest rate risk might affect bank borrowers.[13]

A number of primary areas can be improved: increase interest revenue, reduce interest expense, reduce loan losses, increase interest margin, create opportunity for noninterest income, and reduce operating and other expense. Professor Hempel offers these suggestions:[14]

> Increase interest income by taking more interest-rate risk, but hedge this rate risk with less costly financial futures or swaps.

> Try to systematically control interest expenses by using a pricing model to determine how much the bank can afford to pay on deposits and borrowed funds. If you cannot maintain an adequate spread on deposits or other borrowed funds, do not make the loan; in other words, never bid more for funds than their resale price.

> Attempt to improve control over loan losses through better risk assessment and collection policies and practices. Identify weak loans, and where possible, require the borrower to raise accessory capital from venture capital firms; in other words, do not take venture capital risks where potential return is linked to narrow interest rate spreads.

Try to increase noninterest income by selling more financial products and services on a fee basis. Within the constraints of competitive pressures, raise fees on current services such as safe deposit boxes, returned checks with insufficient balances to cover payment, and so forth.

Achieve better control over noninterest expense—that is, reduce overhead as much as possible. This may have to include some staff cutbacks, subletting extra space in branches to insurers or lawyers, monitoring energy costs, reducing unnecessary travel and entertainment expenses, and eliminating any wasteful expenditures.

Prudent financial management also means avoiding some common errors:[15]

Do not take higher credit risks in an effort to compensate for increasing expenses; do not take security gains prematurely just to increase current net income at a cost to future earnings.

Do not get involved in financial product and service areas in which the bank has no management expertise.

Do not believe that increasing the asset size automatically brings higher earnings; most studies show large diseconomies of scale.

Do not lengthen the portfolio without addressing interest rate sensitivity problems. Doing so is a prescription for disaster.

The Small Bank and Thrift

The stock of a small local or regional bank generally sells for a higher price to earnings ratio and has a higher return on assets and equity than stock of their money center bank counterparts. There are, at most small banks, fewer loan losses and little or no participation in foreign loans. Most of these banks are reasonably well capitalized and should not have to face the burden faced by the giants of having to raise additional capital to meet regulatory requirements. Lack of excess capital among the giant banks can be expected to limit the ability of the large banks to make acquisitions should interstate banking be permitted. This does not mean that the big banks do not want to expand beyond their state lines; it just means that they will be extremely selective about acquisitions and choose locations and targets carefully. In 1984, when many of the large banks filed to charter nonbank banks in an attempt to surmount the interstate banking loophole, no bank filed for more than twenty locations and there were less than 400 applications in total. Many of the applications were concentrated at the most desirable areas, such as Florida, Atlanta, Philadelphia, Los Angeles, Dallas, and Houston.

Many smaller banks have a closer rapport with their customers and know and understand customers' needs better than many of the large money center or regional banks. Frequently, the smaller banks have a lower cost of funds than the bigger banks, a situation created by a lack of competition in some parts of the country. Certainly with more advertising and increased competition, the smaller banks will lose some of their bigger customers in smaller towns, but for the most part, customers tend to remain loyal to smaller local banks. Local banks also tend to have lower personnel costs than their big city counterparts. People tend to remember and respect the local banker who lent money to expand the business or the farm. They also like the personal touch available in many small banks where the customer is known and seen as often by the president as by the teller. The message really is that the small bank should not fear takeover by a giant bank. There may be some takeover attempts by the regional banks wishing to expand within their territory, but stockholders have historically been generously rewarded in those instances where the takeover was successful. In addition, senior management can usually negotiate "golden parachute" contracts to ensure their employment in a merger situation for up to five years. Attractive bank acquisition targets will likely be those banks that serve statewide or regional markets and have strong retail customer bases. Community banks in rural markets are unlikely acquisition candidates.

For those smaller banks that feel the need to be involved with larger banks but still desire independence, there are two other alternatives that come to mind. One is to become part of a regional consortium, while the other is to purchase a franchise or a participation in the computer technology and other correspondent banking services of a larger bank. For example, a number of southern banks located in different states have purchased a 4.9 percent interest in each other. This gives them an opportunity of doing some things in conjunction with each other involving compatible computer, ATM, and correspondent bank services. It also provides for joint lending opportunities to meet loan demand for larger customers that could not be accommodated by any one of the individual banks because of capital constraints. These consortium combinations also provide additional media attention and coverage, which some participants may be able to capitalize on to attract new customers. The consortium gives each bank an indication of what an actual merger might be like down the road. It could also possibly prevent a hostile takeover, which in some instances might have been the original goal of the consortium.

A number of California banks and New York City banks, as well as a few other vendors, have developed home banking systems and comparative shopping and information systems that utilize home computers. Many small banks might wish to offer these useful services. Although the small bank may not have either the technical expertise or the capital to develop the system, it may offer the system either for defensive reasons or to add new customers and fee income from both new and original customer bases. It is possible to buy a franchise into this new technology and other correspondent bank services. Although these videotex-type systems are not anticipated to be necessities in the near term, one-third of U.S. families are expected to have access to them by the year 2000, and they should become an important feature of doing business in the financial services industry in the not-too-distant future. It appears as if networking will represent a key strategy for banks of all sizes in seeking access to new technology. It could become important for small banks to develop proprietary services such as banking at home, point-of-sale credit and debit cards, and linkage to a regional or national ATM network.

Small banks differ from their larger counterparts in some other ways that have not previously been mentioned. Since large and medium-size banks are likely to overlap in competing for so-called middle-market companies, small banks will serve fewer industries and will have to focus on small businesses, the consumer, and mortgage markets. Large and medium-size banks will offer a full range of high-quality, highly automated services internationally, nationally, regionally, and locally in large markets. Smaller banks will offer a narrower range of services and serve only the smaller local markets. In the nature of things, however, there will be some overlap. Small banks will adopt a more personalized, higher-quality image in serving customers, especially in cases and in localities where the larger banks compete. In the main, smaller banks should be successful in their effort to preserve their local geographic niche and should be able to distinguish themselves from their larger competitors.

There appears to be a national trend toward opening new "boutique" banks and savings and loan associations to satisfy consumers' hunger for personal services. These small independent financial institutions are similar to specialty shops. They are generally located in high-growth, affluent areas in which specific services are targeted to certain audiences. Some of these organizations serve small corporations and professionals; others offer their customers a private office in which to do their banking, while others offer club or reading rooms to their best customers. A few banks will even provide a personal courier service to pick up customer deposits.

A number of smaller banks and thrifts specialize in seeking special classes of customers such as women, lawyers, doctors, other professionals, or "upscale" customers. Other customers that can be targeted are ethnic in nature. Banks may court Greek, Cuban, Mexican, Chinese, Japanese, Puerto Rican, or Vietnamese ethnic minorities by locating branches in these ethnic neighborhoods and staffing them with employees who speak both English and the native tongue. Many ethnic-based branches have a larger-than-average percentage of their deposits in lower-cost passbook deposits.

Each small bank or thrift should channel its energies into certain profitable niches. With today's high operating expenses, a small financial institution cannot be all things to all people. Unprofitable services must be eliminated and cost controls must be introduced. For example, unprofitable branches should be sold. The small institution should try to develop more fee services and should consider raising fees on safe deposit boxes, money orders, credit cards, late charges on mortgage payments, wire transfers, foreign drafts and remittances, bond coupon deposits, as well as check fees for nonsufficient balances, uncollected funds, stop payment requests, and certified checks. Mailing costs can be reduced by sending out certificate balance reports only once a year rather than monthly or quarterly. Sorting of mail by zip code prior to mailing and delivering them to the post office can also be helpful in reducing mailing costs. Accounts with low balances should be closed if the costs of servicing these accounts exceeds the benefits to the bank of having the deposit and account relationship. Customers should be asked to raise their balances in their accounts to an agreed on target level before closing an account.

Finding a profitable niche for some thrifts may require entering into joint venture developmental residential real estate activities with builders who have been long-term and dependable customers of the bank. Some thrifts may emphasize mortgage banking activities. Other thrifts and small banks may offer highly personalized services, extended hours, discount brokerage, income tax preparation, trust service, insurance sales, videotex/computerized home banking, and comparative shopping service specialization within the local community. Because of resource constraints, few thrifts will be able to offer all the services in which they are currently permitted involvement.

For a handful of thrift institutions, service corporations have been good profit producers. However, for the savings and loan industry overall, the data indicates that service corporation earnings were neither countercyclical nor the salient contributor to company profitability during 1981 to 1983.[16]

The small bank or thrift must take advantage of its knowledge of local businesses and its close ties to customers. It must profit from its involvement in local real estate. It must continue to foster business and civic relationships within the local community. A bank or a thrift must keep itself open to a potential buy-out and avoid any irreversible steps that might destroy the future marketability of the institution.

Small banks with high operating costs, low return on assets, and insufficient capital may be wise to accept an attractive buy-out offer or to seek a merger partner. A small bank with a return on assets below 0.80 is an institution that does not compare favorably within its peer group. On the other hand, a money center bank with a return on assets at that level would be considered to be doing quite well.

In the case of many thrifts that face net worth problems, there are two possible alternatives: (1) merger and (2) bringing in new capital. The regulatory authorities would be remiss in allowing low-net-worth thrift associations to go public. Troubled institutions should consider finding a friendly association that is interested in a merger. It is likely that key employees will be able to maintain their jobs and that most, but not all, of the acquired entity's employees will be maintained by the acquiring institution. If the regulatory authorities force a merger (unfriendly merger), it is likely that the top officers of the troubled thrift will be forced to resign.

An enterprise with good income prospects and satisfactory net worth can possibly offer stock in public markets and perhaps obtain a wide distribution of geographic ownership. However, there is a risk that conversion from a mutual to a stock-owned thrift can mean change of ownership or dilution of control. Private capital can sometimes be found from friendly hands in the local community.

Stephen A. Rhoades, a staff member of the Federal Reserve Board, in a paper delivered to the American Political Science Association's annual convention in Washington in 1984, examined the possible implications of interstate banking for small banks and local communities. He concluded that small banks

Grow as quickly as large banks in most cases;

Tend to return to the original market share even when bigger banks enter their local market;

Are almost as efficient as large banks and for the most part are more profitable and better capitalized;

Have adapted reasonably well to the new electronic technology in banking, especially in the use of ATMs.[17]

With respect to interstate banking, Rhoades believes that small banks should be able to remain as viable businesses in their local communities. Notwithstanding, it is possible that some small banks will merge voluntarily or be forced into failure or merger by the entry of a vigorous competitor in the local market. The latter case would be the exception rather than the norm and is unlikely to occur unless the local institution is inefficient in its operations and unaggressive in providing and pricing services to customers.[18] In the former case, banks may choose to merge because of an attractive offer and the guarantee of prestigious jobs in the new organization for key employees. Interstate banking might stimulate mergers between smaller banks. Motivation might be to become more attractive acquisition targets, to become large enough to reduce the probability of a takeover, or simply to offer a wider and more complete range of services to a larger geographic region.

Banks and Insurance Companies

According to some analysts, banks have some advantages over insurance companies because:

1. Banks have more frequent contact with their customers than do insurance agents;
2. Bank branch distribution systems are cheaper than a network of agents;
3. The public perceives banks as being more trustworthy than insurance companies.

Many partnerships have been formed between banks and insurers, under which the insurers sell policies in bank lobbies. For example, American International Life Assurance Company leases space from Citibank. Other partnerships include Capital Holding Co. with Bank of America; Travelers Corp. with Hawkeye Bancorp; Aetna Life and Casualty Co. with First Tennessee Bank; Equitable Assurance Society of the United States with Alaska Mutual Bank; ITT Life Insurance Corp. with several banks and thrifts; Nationwide Life Insurance Co. with Bank One. Also, ISFA Corp., which operates the Invest brokerage service for thrifts, will soon offer insurance in its package to subscribers.

Most of these combinations were formed after the Comptroller of the Currency offered the opinion in 1983 that national banks may enter into a percentage lease arrangement with an insurance agency. Rental is usually based on the amount of branch space used and volume generated. Of course, the insurance agency must be identified as an entity independent of the bank, and its office may not be staffed by bank employees.

Banks and insurance companies are beginning to form partnerships for the sale of products and services other than direct insurance sales at bank branch offices. For example, some large banks are reaching regulatory limits on the amount of letters of credit outstanding and want both to increase their volume in this area and to decrease their credit risk. With a well-capitalized, sophisticated participation in the money business, like an insurance company, a partnership is an ideal approach to accomplish this purpose. There are other ways for banks and insurance companies to synergize, such as offering commercial loans and commercial paper with credit enhancement insurance. When an insurance bond guarantees the prompt payment of principal and interest on intermediate corporate notes and commercial paper, banks can sell their loans outright or finance them using innovative techniques without impinging on regulatory limitations. Banks will be able to increase involvement in accounts receivable financing if the obligations are backed by credit insurance. And the business concept is viable because the cost of bank interest plus credit insurance is less than the costs of dealing with a factor.

Insurance companies and their agents should be aggressive in approaching local banks and thrifts to determine how they can work together to enhance their joint profitability. An insurance unit located in a bank branch or participation in a financial risk package jointly by a bank and an insurance company seems to make much sense.

Insurance Company Distribution Trends

Insurance companies will have to find ways to lower their distribution costs and basic overhead because some insurance lines are being treated like commodities. With limited product differentiation, the insurer with the lowest price should be in a position to generate the greatest volume of business. This implies that the efficient, low-cost producer will be at an advantage because insurance coverage will theoretically be sold at the lowest price. At the same time, investment income will become an even more important determinant of insurance company profitability. Insurance companies are expected to pay even more attention to the investment function as companies strive to improve their profitability. More effective flexibility and matching of assets to liabilities are considered salient factors for a productive investment portfolio.

Insurance companies will implement improved information systems that supply current and easily generated information on customers, their relationships, and their characteristics and will use personal computers and word processing systems. They will likely experiment with other distribution systems that do not rely exclusively on independent agents. Insurance companies will establish multifaceted distribution systems that emphasize mass mailings, telephone sales, and offering their products and services in bank and thrift lobbies in order to cut distribution costs. Insurance will be sold on videotex and cable TV systems that are linked to the home computer. Insurance companies and their agents are also expected to attempt more group policy sales arrangements to fraternal organizations, trade and professional associations, trade unions, and credit unions. Insurance companies have continued to purchase brokerage firms in an attempt to have a multiple distribution system and to reach the up-scale consumer. Distribution and marketing seem more critical than structure. The companies that find a method to efficiently distribute multiple financial service products to defined target markets will be among the true winners.

Successful insurance companies will spend more time than heretofore on strategic and long-range planning. They will determine what products and services consumers really want and how to market to them at the lowest possible cost. They will determine what acquisitions should be made and, in some cases, whether a demutualization program is appropriate. Some companies will affiliate with a bank, some with a major retailer, and perhaps some with a supermarket chain. Successful companies will implement long-range and strategic plans that include detailed strategies to achieve specific goals and objectives and will link management compensation to fulfillment of the strategic plans.

Productivity gains will be among the key factors that help improve insurance company earnings. Lowering operating costs is one obvious method of improving productivity, but there are others. Sales productivity should be improved by modifying products and distribution channels and by implementing new or improved automated agency systems, while enhanced productivity in operations should come through further advancement in automation, better training of personnel, and improvement in monitoring programs. An improvement in executive productivity will be created by linking compensation increase to improvement. Responsiveness to the external environment and an effective strategic planning process are among the factors vital to successful management. The successful company will also have to concentrate on retention of policyholders, strong investment performance, and product development skills.[19]

Insurance companies will develop other sources of fee income from subsidiaries involved in brokerage, discount brokerage, mutual funds, and money market funds. There will be more depository products offered to customers, as well as annuities, real estate, and energy-limited partnerships. Larger insurance companies will begin to provide consulting services in risk management to smaller insurance companies and to corporations.

Demutualization of Insurance Companies

A number of studies on the subject of demutualization have been undertaken by major investment banking firms such as Goldman Sachs, Merrill Lynch, and E.F. Hutton. The American Council of Life Insurance is also studying the issue and preparing some guidelines for members. The continued expansion of the insurance industry into banking, brokerage, and investment-related services will lead even that industry to require additional capital to help achieve anticipated external acquisitions and to finance internal growth. A mutual insurance company can fully enhance its capital base by converting to stock form of ownership. It might obtain additional equity capital in an initial public offering of common stock concurrently with demutualization if the regulatory authorities permit. Where this is not possible, an offering of common stock can be made subsequent to conversion. After conversion, an insurance company can raise additional capital through sale of commercial paper, bank borrowings, mortgaging of real estate assets, and public sale of securities other than common stock, such as debentures or preferred stock. Since investors in debt instruments of mutual insurers are subordinated in right of repayment to policyholders, the ability of mutuals to borrow in the debt or money markets is limited.

The advantages of demutualization include:[20]

1. Opportunity for the insurance company to expand its equity base;
2. Opportunity for greater access to capital markets;
3. Ability to facilitate expansion through acquisitions and mergers;

4. Ability to escape certain federal income taxes contained in proposed congressional legislation;
5. Ability to form an upstream holding company that effectively allows the company to participate in business activities outside the purview of the state insurance regulatory agency;
6. Opportunity to attract and offer management new equity-linked incentive compensation plans;
7. Opportunity to stimulate media interest in each phase of the process of converting, which could help a company increase its market penetration by heightening degree of name recognition.

Conversion to stock form has a number of disadvantages that must be considered:[21]

1. Complex accounting, actuarial, valuation, ownership, legal, and tax issues must be resolved.
2. Substantial time is required for an insurer's senior management to analyze the salient issues prior to demutualization, and additional time must be given to shareholders, security analysts, and investment advisors during the lengthy conversion process and thereafter.
3. The process is arduous, complicated, and costly.
4. A stock company has the additional regulatory burden of security law compliance and the expense of shareholder reports, communications, and administration.
5. A stock company could become susceptible to an unfriendly takeover.
6. Management strategy and operating results are subject to greater scrutiny.

Notes

1. S.J. Goldstein, "Thrifts' Question to Hedge or Not to Hedge," *American Banker*, Aug. 21, 1984, p. 24.

2. *Profitability: Do the Pieces Still Fit?*, U.S. League Profitability Seminars, Aug. 1984, p. 93.

3. Goldstein, p. 22.

4. N.H. Rothstein and J.M. Little, "The Market Participants and Their Motivations," *Handbook of Financial Futures* (New York: McGraw-Hill, 1984), p. 125.

5. G. Hecton, "The Thrift Industry Is under Seige Again," *Fortune*, Oct. 15, 1984, pp. 171–81.

6. *Ibid.*

7. J.L. Lincoln and L.G. Dutton, Jr., *Stock Thrifts* (Philadelphia: Packard Press, 1983), p. 1.

8. *Ibid.*, pp. 4, 5.

9. Financial Services Industry Forum, sponsored by Arthur Andersen & Co. and The Institutional Investor, Washington, D.C., June 1984.

10. Bulletin PA-7a-2, Federal Home Loan Bank Board, Washington, D.C., June 6, 1984.

11. *Kaplan-Smith Report,* July 1984, pp. 7–8.

12. *Ibid.*

13. G.H. Hempel, "How to Reverse Poor Performance?," *American Banker,* Oct. 2, 1984, p. 9.

14. *Ibid.,* p. 11.

15. *Ibid.*

16. *Profitability: Do the Pieces Still Fit?,* U.S. League Profitability Seminars, Aug. 1984, p. 50.

17. S.A. Rhoades, "No Threat to Small Banks," *American Banker,* Oct. 11, 1984, p. 19.

18. *Ibid.*

19. *Changing Horizons for Insurance: Charting a Course for Success,* Arthur Andersen & Co. and Life Office Management Association, 1984, p. 2.

20. *Insurance Company Demutualization* (New York: Merrill Lynch Capital Markets, 1984).

21. *Conversion from Mutual to Stock Form* (New York: E.F. Hutton & Co., June 1984).

6
The Future

At this point let us look at the major trends that have taken place within the financial services industry and those that are likely to take place over the next decade:

1. Technology is expected to continue playing a major role in tomorrow's financial services industry. In addition to helping reduce costs and increase productivity, comparative shopping systems will probably assume increased importance in the future via videotex systems and home computers. Many products and services will be available for purchase at large discounts from the so-called retail price via the bank or videotex shopping service. Not only will financial services be offered in these systems, but so will thousands of other products from appliances to automobiles. The consumer will also be able to buy these products and services without leaving the home and pay for them by using debit or credit cards. Also, debit cards, point-of-sale terminals, and check verification systems are expected to gain in usage over the next decade. Banking at home on the computer is also expected to increase in popularity over the next decade, while ATM machines are expected to account for over half of consumer banking transactions. The proliferation and popularity of ATM machines will reduce the need for full-size brick-and-mortar branches and should lead to shorter hours at branches, since the ATMs are available twenty-four hours a day. Most newer branches will be considerably smaller than those currently in operation.

2. Banks will likely account for a respectable percentage of the sale of personal lines insurance by the year 2000. It is unclear whether banks will be able to underwrite insurance or just distribute personal lines insurance products. Most banks probably will have a joint relationship with an insurance company or insurance agency and will offer personal lines products such as life, health, auto, homeowners, and annuities in their lobbies as well as through monthly envelope stuffers in depository and credit card statements. However, if the regulatory authorities permit, some of the larger banks will become underwriters as well as distributors.

3. Insurers fear that the huge customer bases and branch networks of banks will permit banks to sell insurance products at prices lower than what are currently the norm within the insurance industry because banks will have lower distribution costs. Large banks seem eager to add insurance to their array of financial services as a way to add fee income and to capture consumers'

funds while expanding their customer base. Both banks and insurers know that when it comes to money matters, customer loyalty is generally not toward the institution but toward cost, convenience, and service.[1]

4. Mass marketing will play a bigger role in the insurance distribution process as the industry attempts to reduce distribution and marketing costs. Companies will use a variety of marketing systems targeted toward specific classes of business and will not be bound by tradition to one distribution system.[2]

5. Commercial banks and thrift institutions have established discount brokerage operations in a move toward product deregulation. This has helped increase the popularity and public awareness of discount brokerage and has helped generate fee income for these institutions.

6. Insurance companies and financial conglomerates have continued to acquire brokerage firms, while some of the largest nationwide brokerage firms have acquired regional and local firms. Prudential, John Hancock, Penn Mutual, Equitable Life Assurance, and Provident Mutual have been among the insurance companies acquiring brokerage firms, while Sears and American Express have been among the conglomerates acquiring brokerage firms. These acquisitions have been made to reach the upscale consumer in order to cross-sell financial products and services and to better position these firms strategically in a period where distribution systems are changing. Some firms also have moved toward the financial supermarket approach. With the entrenchment of Sears, JCPenney, and Krogers in the financial services industry, we can begin to expect an even bigger role for retailers within the financial services industry.

7. The sale of personal financial services through the home computer should grow rapidly if costs can be effectively reduced. The consumer participating in the new technology may view insurance as a commodity and will tend to be price sensitive. That customer will have direct access to rates of various insurance companies as well as the ability to do comparative shopping for other products and services on the home computer/videotex system.[3]

8. In addition to seeing the continued conversion of mutual thrift institutions into stock-held companies, it is likely that we will enter a period where insurance mutuals will begin the process of demutualization and conversion. However, the process of demutualization of insurance companies is more complex than it is for savings and loans and savings banks, where the regulatory authorities have established guidelines at the federal level.

9. Some form of interstate banking will probably be instituted by the year 2000, and this should substantially reduce the total number of banks. The banking structure may consist largely of regional combinations, consortia of regional banks, franchising, reverse-franchising, or even forms of limited partnerships among banks. It also is possible that future sessions of Congress will resolve the nonbank bank loophole and require some retroactive

divestiture. With the interstate mergers and acquisitions of failing banks and thrifts, we have taken another step toward interstate banking. Also, a number of interstate mergers have been authorized among regional banks located in New England and the southeastern part of the United States. The growth of electronic funds transfers, interstate networks of ATMs, interstate advertising by large banks to acquire deposits, national loan production offices, and Edge Act offices, as well as the establishment of nationwide finance companies and other acquisitions under the holding company umbrella, offer still other channels for achieving interstate banking.

10. Certain other forms of nationwide banking affiliations might develop through "reverse franchise" consortia or limited partnerships for groups of banks. In the former case, the organizing banks would form a central authority that might then develop nationwide telecommunications and systems linkages and nationwide banking services for marketing by its members. Since the franchisees are forming their own captive franchisor, all of the operating earnings of the central authority would flow back to the member banks instead of to a third party. In the limited partnership arangement, a number of banks could become limited partners, with the general partner being a nonbanking company with a data processing and telecommunications background. In this way, banks could form a nationwide network and provide the bases for developing centralized treasury services. By pooling resources the member banks would retain their autonomy while enjoying the leveraging effects that national coverage and large-scale operations currently offer to some of the money center banks.[4]

11. Some analysts expect the number of independent insurance agents to decline dramatically by the year 2000 as banks enter into at least the distribution of personal lines insurance, as mass marketing increases, and as the telecommunications/home computer/videotex industry offers comparative insurance shopping at home without the services of an agent. If banks sell insurance and if insurance is available via comparative shopping-at-home systems, the independent agent who restricts sales to just personal lines runs a risk of losing price conscious customers. Agents should sell commercial insurance lines, as well as additional personal line products such as annuities, mutual funds, money market funds, and tax shelters in order to achieve continual contact with their customers and help to retain their personal lines clients.

Banks are looking for quick, easy sales and not the in-depth, fact-finding, and lengthy presentations that are the forte of the independent agent. While banks will participate in insurance sales via envelope stuffers in monthly statements and credit card billings, the aggressive independent agent can do the same with billings as well as other target mailings to various association members or retail stores credit card customers. The agent can also reach prospects by phone.[5]

12. The insurance industry is also moving toward greater fee and consultation income, as companies act increasingly as risk-management advisers and counselors to corporate clients and become more actively engaged in external money management.

13. We can expect to see more financial institutions utilize the futures and options market for hedging in an attempt to offset interest rate risks and to better balance maturities or roll-over dates in their asset and liability management positions.

14. On the regulatory front, even if banks are not permitted by Congress to underwrite insurance in 1985, large banks can be expected to succeed in pressing Congress to enact legislative changes before the end of the decade. Also, New York banks will continue to exert pressure on their state legislature to authorize bank underwriting of insurance at least in New York.

15. Capital requirements for commercial banks and thrifts are likely to increase, which should "play well in Peoria" and lead to an increase in public confidence in the banking system. However, increases could hold back the growth rate of money center banks, which would be affected most by their below-average capitalization ratios. At the same time, bankers are developing strategies to minimize their need for added capital. We can also expect a change in deposit insurance premiums paid by banks and thrifts. Deposit premiums will most likely be determined by some form of variable charges that reflect differences in risk.

16. Key factors for success in retail deposit-taking are expected to remain high interest rates and convenient location or access. Perceived institutional safety will increase in importance, while customer/bank relationships should become less important.

17. In a rapidly changing environment, banks that are constrained by systems inadequacies could lose a substantial competitive edge and could face difficulty in obtaining productivity gains to counter shrinking profits. While ease of access is still an important feature for a retail depositor in selecting a bank, convenient access is no longer defined solely by branch location. Banks will have to deploy a combination of physical and technological facilities to achieve maximum penetration while containing fixed costs. The banking business has become increasingly market and customer driven. Banks will have to begin to build a far more substantial base of market intelligence. Banks must develop marketing programs that carefully respond to the needs of each market segment, and they must educate customers as to the merits of new services such as ATMs, POS debit cards, and home banking, where consumer demand is not inherently strong. Successful banks must not only identify potentially profitable market segments, but they must also be able to capture adequate and profitable market share through superior products, lower costs and prices, or high barriers to competitive entry.[6]

18. Equity participations in commercial lending should become a routine banking practice by 1990. Other commercial lending trends will include a reduced emphasis on compensating balances, more explicit pricing, and greater use of hedging of fixed-rate loans.

19. A 1983 survey by the Federal Reserve Bank of Atlanta found that two-thirds of major grocery and convenience store operators in the Southeast either already had ATMs or had plans to install them on their premises. Most of the retailers felt that ATMs promised distinct advantages in attracting customers, reducing problems with bad checks, and expanding their range of customer services. In addition, the ATM was often viewed as a steppingstone to the point-of-sale cash register terminal and the debit card.[7]

Grocery and convenience stores are particularly important in the evolution of POS terminals and the debit card because these stores cash an unusually large number of checks and need a faster and cheaper means to negotiate such payments and to eliminate bad checks. Essentially, the traditional retail payment system has become a burden, with supermarkets spending huge sums on check processing costs. Convenience stores are also concerned with eliminating currency in cash registers, which should discourage robberies.[8] The bottom line is going to be a rapidly growing use of both POS terminals, check verification systems, and debit cards.

20. Some observers expect to see a rapid nationalization of the mortgage market. What the proponents of the nationalization of mortgage markets envision is a finance system that circumvents the traditional home lending function of savings institutions. The thrifts would be left to provide mortgage banking or commercial banking functions. Traditionally, the major source of mortgage funds has been savings institutions. Small commercial banks and some of the larger ones have also been originators of home mortgages. Mortgage bankers originate but generally do not hold mortgage loans and usually depend on secondary market sales. It is interesting to note that many thrifts and commercial banks or their holding companies own mortgage banking operations. The secondary market then packages mortgage loans into securities that are then sold by the investment banking community to investors. A salient element in this process has been the participation of FNMA, FHLMC, and GNMA (Government National Mortgage Association), which have provided loan packaging and the federal credit agency guarantee. "Like the theater actor who, when tested on center stage moves from understudy to star, so, too, the secondary mortgage market has captured the limelight in real estate finance."[9] It is also important to note that realtors and home builders have increased significantly their involvement in the mortgage origination process in the last few years.[10]

21. As a traditionally local real estate business goes increasingly national, real estate brokers are linking up with innovative real estate franchisors

less for image purposes than for tangible fees involved in financing, insuring, or investing in property. Some franchisors do this on their own, while others work with traditional financial service firms eager to get closer to the 2 to 4 million resales of existing homes every year.

Some savings and loans have joined a four-way partnership with local franchisees, mortgage companies, and real estate companies. Real estate brokers will earn fees for originating loans for member thrifts, which in turn would be able to use mortgage company financial programs if they lack funds for mortgages. It is possible that thrifts and key brokers will operate from desks in each other's offices as a "natural alliance of the brokerage business, the primary seller of real estate, and the savings and loan industry, the primary financier," according to T.H. Pitt, Jr., president of Home Savings Association of Rocky Mount, North Carolina.[11] In addition, some real estate franchisors such as Century 21 have started departments within its larger offices to handle insurance, mortgage finance, commercial real estate brokerage, as well as property syndication and management.

22. It is anticipated that savings and loan associations will depend more on money and capital markets as a source of funds as deposit rate controls are phased out. This could lead to a higher cost of funds and a dominance of variable-rate mortgages offered to the public in order to avoid the interest rate risk of owning fixed-rate mortgages. Members of the thrift industry will become more diversified in terms of the mix of both assets and liabilities and will have to become more profit-oriented and liquidity-conscious if they are to survive. Many of the largest institutions are operating on a multistate basis. It is hoped that economies of scale will result from increased size. Out-of-state loan production offices or branches on a regional or national basis will be utilized by the largest and strongest of these institutions.

23. Some experts foresee a thrift industry with:

a. Some savings and loan associations that evolve into one-stop family financial centers or supermarkets that will offer NOW accounts, credit cards, telephone transfer accounts, bill-payer accounts, improved electronic funds transfer services, mortgage and consumer loans, and other consumer services;

b. Other savings and loan associations that offer more specialized real estate services that may emphasize lending to industrial and commercial organizations in the form of short-term construction, acquisition, and development loans;

c. Other thrifts that emulate mortgage bankers with their focus on secondary market activities, such as the buying, selling, and servicing of mortgages as a source of profits instead of originating mortgages for addition to the portfolio;

d. Large thrifts that form thrift-controlled financial conglomerates that might include, for example, insurance companies, brokerage firms, and mortgage banking companies.

24. The trend toward larger financial institutions and the formation of financial conglomerates is likely to continue. However, there will still be room for the financial boutique, specialty shop, and firm that offers the customer professional and personalized treatment.

25. According to an Atlanta Federal Reserve Bank survey, affluent consumers, who use the greatest variety of financial services, are generally reluctant to consolidate their services. Most U.S. households currently prefer to continue obtaining insurance from insurance companies, brokerage services from brokerage firms, and banking services from banks. However, some consumers would like to have all these businesses located in a single place. The segment of the population most amenable to consolidating these financial services into one institution is heavily weighted with young, low- to middle-income consumers, and those in the age 50 to 64 group. However, the upscale segment is the least likely to be attracted by consolidation.[12]

26. Consumers might change their buying habits for financial services only to the extent that creative marketing can convince consumers to change their buying patterns. Current patterns show that most consumers patronize specialists for their financial needs. While many customers will continue to do so, those consumers who want to save money, time, and effort will have the opportunity to do so at some financial supermarkets and videotex systems. Those corporations with the means to provide similar quality service, knowledge, and good prices under one roof could possibly benefit from full financial service availability.[13]

27. The survey data are not conclusive but give the impression that the general population's current demand for additional product deregulation is not great. Educating consumers regarding the availability of these offerings and permitting them to become accustomed to obtaining them from a single location might reduce some resistance. Still, some firms do not believe the effort worthwhile when it comes to staff training and overall preparation required to offer all these services.

28. Major consolidation is expected among the approximately 18,000 banks and thrifts. Many of the remaining banks will be strained to finance normal expansion from retained earnings, leaving little to finance external expansion. With the increases in capital requirements announced by bank regulators, many banks will be limited by a basic lack or scarcity of capital for external growth. Also, as long as bank shares have quoted market prices at or below their book value, raising capital through new stock issues is not particularly appealing. Also, joint ventures can be used to economize on scarce capital, so the branch or bank earns fee income. It is of course possible for some of the giant banks to develop national bank networks without branches. Since banks play

such a unique role in the payments system, they are likely to play a key role in the consolidation of financial services. Their actions will of course be guided by remaining regulatory restraints.[14]

29. The number of foreign financial institutions involved in the U.S. market has grown rapidly. For example, foreign banks in the United States have had their assets grow from $7 billion in 1965 to $324 billion by midyear 1983. Foreign banks are attracted to the United States because of their need for dollars as well as the size of the U.S. banking market. Although on a much more limited scale, foreign insurers have also begun to enter the U.S. market, particularly in the reinsurance marketplace. These trends are likely to continue. In addition, technology has played a salient role in facilitating the internationalization of financial services.

30. Bank trust departments are expected to expand their traditional role of serving only the wealthy. They will begin to target younger affluent households, professionals, and private businesses.

31. One by-product of deregulation may well be more financial disclosure requirements for banks. A.A. Sommer, Jr., a former Securities and Exchange commissioner, has argued that greater information and disclosure will result in better bank management because bankers know that their actions will be scrutinized more closely. "As deregulation goes forward, the only adequate substitute for it is disclosure, so that . . . the public becomes the effective regulator of the banks."[15]

32. The individual life insurance industry has become a key target in the move toward diversification. The industry is perceived as a growth industry that is vulnerable to competition because of its[16]

a. High costs and inefficient distribution systems;
b. High profit margins on most of its products with price competition blunted by complex products that are not particularly easy to compare;
c. Vulnerability to a raid on the existing life insurance coverage in force and to replacement with products that cost less;
d. The perception that many companies within the industry are captives of their own distribution system and may be poorly positioned to compete through alternative distribution systems that are likely to emerge.

Of course, holders of equity positions in the company to be acquired may benefit substantially from an acquisition, while some key employees may lose their jobs as companies try to cut costs, overhead, and duplication of jobs in the combined company.

33. Problems of inefficiency continue to plague all insurance companies. Every company is being forced to cut expenses of operation (distribution, administration of underwriting, and administration of claims) from as much as 55 percent in some companies to as little as 17 percent in the most efficient direct-selling companies. Reductions in expenses may be achieved through[17]

a. Additional mass marketing approaches;
b. Expanded use of direct billing;
c. Increased agency automation and multiple company interfacing;
d. Expanded company interdepartmental automation;
e. Use of continuous coverage (automatically renewable) policies;
f. Elimination of current duplication of work between company and agency;
g. Payroll deduction, credit cards and debit cards, and other ease-of-payment plans for personal lines coverage;
h. Full realization of paperless operation of companies and agencies alike.

34. More investment-oriented insurance products are expected. The universal/variable life products are expected to emerge as the market share leaders, with traditional whole life policy sales expected to decline about 5 percent per year in annual sales volume through 1990. We can expect to see more adjustable life insurance policies that let policyholders adjust a policy's face amount, change the period of coverage, and raise or lower premiums as their needs change. Policyholders will be able to switch from one product to another without penalty. This trend is expected to produce a shorter product life cycle of five to seven years.[18]

35. Insurance companies are expected to offer financial counseling, brokerage service, home mortgages, commercial loans, centralized cash-management accounts, or savings accounts. It is expected that more than 60 percent of life companies will provide financial counseling services and mutual/money market funds by 1990. Between 30 and 60 percent of life companies are expected to offer home mortgages, security brokerage, and property/casualty insurance.[19]

36. Within property/casualty commercial lines we may see[20]

a. More intense competition among existing companies, captives, life insurance companies, and foreign insurers;
b. More self-insurance and risk retention as well as the use of higher deductibles;
c. Greater emphasis on safety and loss control programs;
d. Policies designed to cover unusual exposure created by new technologies;
e. Combined single policy comprehensive coverage for worker's compensation, accidental death and dismemberment, and long-term disability;
f. Greater care in pricing products, improved loss control and expense control, and better claims handling.

37. We will begin to see package policies combining previously separate lines of insurance, in addition to existing combinations of separate perils. For example, Continental Insurance Co. has a policy called Comprehensive Protection that combines homeowners, personal umbrella, and auto insurance with options such as disability income and mortgage life insurance. Insurance

companies are expected to make every effort to tie clients to their company with unique combinations of coverage, easy payment plans, risk-management advice, and quick and convenient claims handling. In combining currently separate lines of coverage (automobile, life, health, and homeowners) under one combination policy, with monthly or quarterly payments, the consumer will probably find it difficult to compare costs of coverage. However, it is still expected that most people will end up buying only one policy to protect against virtually all losses.[21]

38. There may be a new way for thrifts to raise relatively inexpensive long-term deposits if an idea of the trust department of First City National Bank of Houston takes hold. The bank has unveiled a new investment for pension funds with a guaranteed yield of 4 percent above the inflation rate for thirty years in FSLIC insured CDs issued by savings and loans, which will be able to be traded in the secondary market. This could possibly touch off a boom in inflation-indexed pension investments, since many pension funds have been criticized for their failure to match a 4 percent real return over the last thirty years.

39. It will become even more difficult during the 1990s to distinguish between Citicorp, Bank of America, American Express, Merrill Lynch, and Prudential and some of the largest thrifts when it comes to retail financial services provided to the consumer.

40. There are likely to be at least three large power bases after the continued consolidation of the financial services industry. Established banks will represent one power base, and established insurers should represent another. The third large power base will come from the customer-oriented organizations that have access to large numbers of potential customers, such as Sears, Merrill Lynch, Kroger, JCPenney, and American Express.[22]

41. How will customer interface of the future actually be structured? Some analysts think that location selling and servicing will become the norm in the financial services industry and point to Sears, Kroger, and JCPenney financial centers and branch banks as likely prototypes. Other analysts visualize a world of banks without branches that increasingly rely on media advertising, credit and debit cards, ATMs, and home computers connected with modems, telephone lines, or cable television. Some imagine that customer interface will take place more and more at the place of employment with a complete extension of the concept of employee benefits. There will of course still be opportunities for financial boutiques to provide personal attention and professional guidance in their chosen specialties. These specialty organizations will serve the specific needs of various market sectors.[23]

42. Among the keys to success in the broad retail market for financial services in the 1990s will be efficient customer access and cost-efficient distribution systems. One compelling reason to consolidate financial services is the economies that would flow if the customer contact could be maintained

on a continuing basis rather than on an occasional basis. We all know that prospecting is extremely time consuming for life insurance agents. If customer access could be achieved through an intermediary prepared to address various financial service needs of potential customers, the frequent contact should increase the possibility of finding a customer needing a particular service.[24]

43. In a Delphi study published in 1983, Arthur Anderson & Co. and the Bank Administration Institute have drawn the following conclusions regarding the future of the financial services industry:[25]

a. The number of banks is expected to decline by about one-third in 1990 to approximately 9,600 banks, with attrition greatest among small banks, which are expected to experience a 41 percent decline in number to 7,800.

b. Bank assets are expected to be more concentrated in large institutions (holding over $1 billion in assets). Their share will account for 65 percent of industry assets, while the share of small banks (under $100 million in assets) is expected to decline to 12 percent.

c. Technology will have an evolutionary, rather than a revolutionary, impact on the banking industry. Home banking is expected to be used by about 10 percent of households in 1990, but 20 to 50 percent of banks will offer it to prevent competitors from gaining a market advantage. Also, the profitability of home banking is questionable because of high start-up costs and uncertain market potential.

d. By 1990, ATMs should surpass human tellers in terms of the share of retail deposit and withdrawal transactions processed, while point-of-sale debit cards are expected to be accepted by 20 percent of households.

e. Bank return on assets is expected to decline about 10 percent by 1990 because of higher deposit costs, increased competition and increased expenses associated with developing new products. Although fee-based income is expected to double, it will still represent only 7 percent of total revenues.

44. Arthur Anderson & Co. and the Life Office Management Association (LOMA) announced the results of a 1984 survey of life insurance executives. Some of the results that concern the future of the life insurance industry include the following:[26]

a. Insurance company executives foresee a shakeout in the industry that could spell the end for many small companies and force the survivors to follow the lead of banks and brokerage houses in providing a broader range of financial services. By 1990, 41 percent (or 350) of all small life insurance companies are expected to merge or be acquired by larger companies.

b. Most companies plan to provide agents with electronic access to home office systems by 1990. This will allow agents to produce illustrations for sales support, answer policyholder inquiries, and submit applications electronically. These tools should allow agents to expand their services, play broader investment-counseling roles, and provide better service to customers.

c. Agent service, price of the policy per amount of coverage, and prior relationship with the selling institution were considered to be the most important factors in influencing a consumer's decision to buy life insurance. Agents will have a larger selection of products to sell, including more equity/investment-oriented products.

d. Captive and independent agent forces should continue to represent the most important distribution methods in the near future, with each generating about 28 percent of total premiums. Sales through owned or franchised brokerage channels were expected to gain between a 15 and 19 percent share of the life insurance market by 1990. The sale of life insurance by banks was expected to be at 9 percent of the market, while direct-mail sales were expected to capture 8 percent of the marketplace by 1990. Surprisingly, sales through home service (debit) agents or videotex and retailers were expected to be negligible by 1990. However, policyholders will be able to make payment with credit cards and to buy insurance through their home computers.

Summary

Many uncertainties lie ahead for the financial services industry. We really do not know what legislation will be passed by Congress relating to product or geographic deregulation or whether enough consumers will participate in the videotex/home computer services to make them profitable for the venders offering the service. It is too early to assess whether these systems represent harbingers of change in the way financial services will be sold or marketed in the United States and abroad or whether insurance agents specializing in personal lines will lose a substantial portion of their market share because of these technological developments.

Many of the much-talked-about advances in technology will proceed slowly, driven more by competition than consumer demand. Despite reticence on the part of consumers, much of the industry plans to pursue this market, largely out of fear that if they do not act, they will lose market share.

On the other hand, it does appear likely that many thrifts and some insurance companies will convert from mutuals to stock-owned companies, that there will be a continued trend toward financial conglomeration and the cross-selling of financial products and services, and that there will always remain a place for the discriminating financial boutique dealing with the upscale customer within the financial services industry. We are also likely to witness the continued trend of a large number of bank and thrift failures or forced mergers, as the shakeout from

1. Three severe recessions in one decade;
2. Extreme interest rate fluctuations;
3. Poor management decision making and controls; and
4. Too much deregulation in too short a period of time.

The insurance industry will also face problems in addition to the bankruptcies of Baldwin United and Charter Co. Inefficient and underreserved insurance and reinsurance companies from within the property and casualty segment of the industry may begin to fail after suffering through six consecutive years of underwriting losses.

In a June 1984 Financial Services Industry Forum, Lawrence A. Weinbach of Arthur Anderson & Co. called the current business environment "turbulent": The "only certainty is that more uncertainty is still in the offing." At the same conference Harvey Shapiro, of *Institutional Investor*, stated that "the old order is breaking down, but we don't know what the new order will look like," while Bruce K. MacLaury, president of the Brookings Institution, felt that financial institutions were "shell-shocked by the rapid pace of structural change within their industry, and . . . yearn(ed) for some of the quieter days of segmented markets."[27]

In response to the rapid change taking place within the industry, John Cox has advised senior managements of financial service companies to remain "flexible" because "failure to do so may make your financial services products the smokestacks of the 1990's." Cox also urged firms to exercise cost discipline, to focus on attractive market segments, and to avoid wasting resources in an attempt to prevent change.[28]

Edward E. Furash of Furash & Co. suggested two other skills that are essential for financial service firms: "the ability to undertake successful mergers and to achieve economies of scale. . . . Economies of scale appear only when management has the tenacity to cut costs, to reduce staff, to make no foolish promise to those acquired, and to force the merger of technology."[29]

It is going to be a challenge for the planners and top managements of our insurance companies, thrifts, and banks to guide their companies through an uncertain and potentially troublesome period for the remainder of this decade. It will require greater strategic, product, and market planning, improved information systems, better cost controls, and superior insights and investment skills to survive and prosper.

Notes

1. L. Brandon, *Sound a Clear Call,* CPCU, (Malvern, Pa.: Harry J. Loman Foundation, 1984), p. 89.

2. *Ibid.,* p. 103.

3. *Ibid.,* p. 102.

4. E.J. Laka, "Pooling Resources Could Put Small Banks Back in Big Game," *American Banker,* Oct. 5, 1984, pp. 4–5.

5. A. Gart, "The Tenacious Contenders," *Viewpoint,* Spring 1984, p. 7.

6. *New Dimensions in Banking: Managing the Strategic Position,* Arthur Anderson & Co. and Bank Administration Institute, 1983.

7. H. Stacy and W.N. Cox, "In Store ATMs," *Economic Review* (Federal Reserve Bank of Atlanta), Jan. 1984, p. 31.

8. *Ibid.,* pp. 32, 41.

9. M.J. Reidy, *Savings Institutions,* Jan. 1984, S–104.

10. *Profitability: Do the Pieces Still Fit?,* U.S. League Profitability Seminars, Aug. 1984, p. 157.

11. "Selling Financial Services from the Real Estate Office," *Business Week,* Oct. 15, 1984, p. 161.

12. V. Bennett, "Consumer Demand for Product Deregulation," *Economic Review* (Federal Reserve Bank of Atlanta), May 1984, p. 34.

13. Brandon, p. 90.

14. J.C. Anderson, "Metamorphosis in Financial Services," *National Underwriter,* Sept. 22, 1984, no. 38, pp. 42–43.

15. *Financial Services Industry Forum Summary Paper,* sponsored by Arthur Anderson & Co. and Institutional Investor, Washington, D.C., June 1984, pp. 11–12.

16. Anderson, pp. 6–7.

17. Brandon, p. 110.

18. *Changing Horizons for Insurance: Charting a Course for Success,* Arthur Anderson & Co. and Life Office Management Association, 1984, pp. 12–13.

19. *Ibid.,* p. 8.

20. Brandon, pp. 94–95.

21. *Ibid.,* pp. 84–85.

22. Anderson, pp. 42–43.

23. *Ibid.,* p. 47.

24. *Ibid.,* p. 42.

25. *New Dimensions in Banking: Managing the Strategic Position.*

26. K. Askew, "Industry Survey: Projections to 1990," *National Underwriter,* Sept. 22, 1984, pp. 3, 20.

27. *Financial Services Industry Forum* (see note 15 above), pp. 49, 50, 55.

28. *Ibid.,* p. 16.

29. *Ibid.,* p. 56.

Index

About the Author

Alan Gart is consultant for Hamilton Reliance Savings Association and is president of Alan Gart, Inc., a Huntingdon Valley, Pennsylvania, consulting company. Dr. Gart is on the board of directors of Copenhagen Reinsurance of America and Provident Mutual Variable Life Co. A regular participant in numerous conferences, he has served as a consultant for Hayden Stone, the Department of the Navy, Manufacturers Hanover Trust Company, PSFS, INA Capital Advisors, and CIGNA Corporation, among others. He is a frequent contributor to business and professional journals, book reviews, and monthly economic newsletters. Dr. Gart, who received his Ph.D. from the University of Pennsylvania, has also been senior vice president and chief investment officer at Parkway Management Corp. and senior vice president at the Girard Bank, vice president at Manufacturers Hanover Trust Company, chief economist at INA Corporation, and professor of finance and international business at Florida International University. He is the author of *The Insider's Guide to the Financial Services Revolution* (McGraw-Hill, 1984).